KV-039-409

ESSENTIAL PSYCHOLOGY

General Editor
Peter Herriot

— EI —

PSYCHOLOGY AND WORK

ESSENTIAL

PSYCHOLOGY

PSYCHOLOGY AND WORK

**D. R. Davies and
V. J. Shackleton**

Methuen

First published 1975 by Methuen and Co Ltd
11 New Fetter Lane, London EC4P 4EE
© 1975 D. R. Davies and V. J. Shackleton
Printed in Great Britain by
Richard Clay (The Chaucer Press), Ltd
Bungay, Suffolk

ISBN (hardback) 0 416 82280 0
ISBN (paperback) 0 416 82290 8

We are grateful to Grant McIntyre of Open Books Publishing Ltd
for assistance in the preparation of this series

Contents

Acknowledgements

We should like to thank Margaret Shackleton and Ann Taylor, Guy Cumberbatch and Bert and Irma Davies for their advice, help and encouragement. We are also grateful to Diana Dyer, Margaret Frape and Rita Benford who typed the manuscript speedily and efficiently.

The Publisher and the authors would also like to thank the Editor of *Applied Ergonomics* for permission to reprint Figures 3.1 and 3.2.

D. R. Davies

V. J. Shackleton

Editor's Introduction

D. R. Davies and V. J. Shackleton have written the introductory text to Unit E of *Essential Psychology*. Many of us have firmly-held views on such questions as: What motivates people to work? How best can one decide whether a person is suited to a job, or a job to a person? What are the best ways of teaching and learning the skills required for a job? This book presents enough of the available evidence to show that these questions are not answerable in such a simple form. It leads ideally on to the more specialized books in the unit.

Unit E of *Essential Psychology* deals with a particular area of applied psychology: psychology and work. This is an ideal topic to demonstrate the ways in which the different psychological models of man and their associated findings can be utilized. The human being as processor of information copes with varied inputs in his job and has to adjust his behaviour accordingly. As a social being, he is much affected by the groups of people with whom he works and the organization within which he operates. As a developing person, his changing view of himself will partly consist of his view of himself at work. As an individual, he brings differing skills and motives to his work. Above all, as a human being, he possesses the capacity to change his work situation to suit his own abilities and objectives.

Essential Psychology as a whole is designed to reflect this changing structure and function of psychology. The authors are both academics and professionals, and their aim has been to introduce the most important concepts in their areas to beginning students. They have tried to do so clearly, but have not attempted to conceal the fact that concepts that now appear central to their work may soon be peripheral. In other words, they have presented psychology as a developing set of views of man, not as a body of received truth. Readers are not intended to study the whole series in order to 'master the basics'. Rather, since different people may wish to use different theoretical frameworks for their own purposes, the series has been designed so that each title stands on its own. But it is possible that if the reader has read no psychology before, he will enjoy individual books more if he has read the introduction (A1, B1 etc.) to the units to which they belong. Readers of the units concerned with applications of psychology (E, F) may benefit from reading all the introductions.

A word about references in the text to the work of other writers – e.g. 'Smith (1974)'. These occur where the author feels he must acknowledge an important concept or some crucial evidence by name. The book or article referred to will be listed in the References (which doubles as Name Index) at the back of the book. The reader is invited to consult these sources if he wishes to explore topics further.

We hope you enjoy psychology.

Peter Herriot

I
Introduction

By definition, work is a central feature of modern industrial society. It occupies much of the time available to most people for the majority of their lives and the economic rewards obtained from it determine an individual's standard of living and, to a considerable extent, his social status. As a recent review of a book on worker dissatisfaction stated, 'the experience of everyday life tells us that the work we do is of first importance – it takes half of our waking lives, steers us to particular social circles, generates daily troubles or triumphs, and defines our political interests and personal identities' (Seeman, 1974).

This book is a brief and selective introductory account to some of the ways in which psychology has attempted to increase our understanding of work behaviour. Many different branches of psychology have contributed to the study of work, including experimental, social and occupational psychology, as have other disciplines such as anatomy, physiology, economics, sociology and engineering. Experimental psychology, traditionally the study of such processes as learning, memory and perception (see A1), has influenced the development of ergonomics (also known as human factors or human engineering) which has been much concerned with problems of work design, the effects of the physical environment upon work behaviour, the improvement of training procedures and the prevention of accidents. Social psychology has drawn attention to the numerous influences of the social environment upon job performance and satisfaction with work. Occupational psychology has amassed a large number of assessment techniques for evaluating occupational preferences, aptitudes, abilities and skills, as well as personality traits, which have been used for the purposes of selection and guidance.

The plan of this book is as follows: in this first chapter we shall look briefly at definitions of work, at the economic and demographic background and at changing conceptions of man at work. In Chapter 2 we examine some of the factors involved in satisfaction and performance at work and in Chapter 3 three approaches to work design are considered, ergonomics, intrinsic motivation and socio-technical systems. In Chapter 4 we discuss selection and guidance and in Chapter 5 training. In Chapter 6 the organizational setting in which work behaviour takes place is surveyed and in the final chapter, Chapter 7, some of the employment problems faced by older workers are outlined and the impact of retirement is described.

Definitions of work

Perhaps one of the simplest definitions of work is that it is the means whereby the goods and services that society desires are produced; such a definition emphasizes the instrumental nature of work. A more complete definition is that 'work ... is an instrumental activity carried out by human beings, the object of which is to preserve and to maintain life, and which is directed at a planful alteration of certain features of man's environment' (Neff, 1968). A broader definition still is that 'work is an activity that produces something of value for other people' (O'Toole, 1973).

However, work also serves various functions for the individual, contributing in particular to self-esteem in two main ways. Firstly, through work an individual can acquire mastery over himself and the environment. Secondly, by engaging in activities which produce goods and services that are valued by others, the individual is able to check his evaluation of himself against others' evaluation of him and thus gain a sense of personal worth. However, as Fromm (1971) has written, 'since modern man experiences himself both as the seller and as the commodity to be sold on the market, his self-esteem depends on conditions beyond his control. If he is successful, he is valuable; if he is not, he is worthless'.

Clearly, then, work may be defined not only in terms of its function in society but also in terms of its significance for the individual worker. As we shall see in the following sections of this chapter, patterns of working – in particular, the relative prevalence of different types of work – within society have varied greatly from one society to another and within a society from time to time, most notably with the advent of industrialization; and conceptions of the role of work in the life of the individual have also, and to some extent correspondingly, changed.

The economic and demographic background

Over the past century or so, the population of most industrialized countries has risen dramatically, and currently the populations of underdeveloped countries are increasing even more rapidly. At the same time, technological change has transformed the range and kind of employment opportunities available in industrialized countries; no doubt, eventually, the same kind of transformation will be apparent in underdeveloped countries.

As Allen (1970) points out, 'the idea of progressive economic development is modern', since up until the last few decades of the eighteenth century, 'technical change was so slow as to justify a charge of stagnation, and the very conception of an ever-expanding economy was alien to the thoughts of the mass of men'. Since that time, however, the application of scientific knowledge and technological expertise to the production of goods and services has made possible the enjoyment of a reasonable rate of economic expansion by most industrialized countries; moreover the rising expectations of steadily growing populations have made it necessary.

But some countries have shown higher growth rates than others, and Denison (1967) surveys some possible reasons for differences in economic expansion between countries. Among these he includes the size of the economy and of the markets

11

available to its products, structural differences between economies (for instance, the percentage of the labour force employed in agriculture or the percentage of women in the labour force), the educational level of the labour force, the application of knowledge derived from scientific and technological research and the amount and kind of capital investment.

Since the end of the Second World War Britain's per capita gross domestic product has been steadily rising. Between the years 1950–57 it grew at an annual rate of 1.7 per cent, between 1957–65 at a rate of 2.4 per cent and between 1963–70 at a rate of 2.7 per cent (Donaldson, 1973). As Donaldson indicates, not only is this last figure a great improvement on prevailing growth rates in the nineteenth century, including the period after the Industrial Revolution, but, since growth takes place at a compound rate, an annual growth rate of 2.7 per cent is sufficient to double the national output within twenty-five years. However the answer to differential rates of economic growth may be framed, it is clear that the disposition of the labour force a century ago was very different in the majority of industrialized countries from its present state. Some industries have declined, others have grown, some occupations have virtually disappeared and new ones have emerged. For example, in the United Kingdom in 1971, less than 2 per cent of the labour force were engaged in agriculture, forestry and fishing, less than 2 per cent in mining and quarrying, about 6 per cent in construction, about 36 per cent in manufacturing and about 54 per cent in service industries (*Social Trends*, 1973). In 1870, the percentages for the first two categories combined were about 52 per cent, for the third and fourth about 23 per cent and for the last about 25 per cent, much of which was made up by domestic service. Over this 100 year period, the size of the labour force rose from 12.8 millions (m) to 24.5m. Even in 1951, 5 per cent of the 23.2m-strong labour force was employed in agriculture, forestry and fishing, 4 per cent in mining and quarrying, 6 per cent in construction, 38 per cent in manufacturing and 47 per cent in service industries. Quite clearly, the service industries are growing most rapidly, particularly the sector concerned with professional and scientific services (Caston, 1973). During the period since 1951 the proportion of women (particularly married women) in the labour force rose from 32 per cent in 1951 to 36 per cent in 1971, and is predicted to rise still further, to 38 per cent, by 1981. In 1951, married women comprised only 14 per cent of the work force. This percentage had increased to 34 per cent in 1971.

Changes in the composition of the work force have been even more dramatic in the United States. In the USA in 1900, 41 per cent of the 28.7m-strong labour force were employed in the extraction industries (agriculture, forestry, fishing and mining), 28 per cent in manufacturing industries and 31 per cent in service industries. In 1960, with a labour force of 68.9m, 10 per cent were employed in extraction industries, 32 per cent in manufacturing industries and 58 per cent in service industries. At the same time, the size of firms has tended to become larger and the ratio of 'managers' to those actually engaged in 'productive activities' has tended to increase.

In the light of such changes, some authorities have begun to speak of the 'post-industrial society', described as 'a knowledge society in a double sense: first, the sources of innovation are increasingly derivative from research and development (and more directly, there is a new relation between science and technology because of the centrality of theoretical knowledge); second, the weight of the society – measured by the proportion of Gross National Product and a larger share of employment – is increasingly in the knowledge field' (Bell, 1974).

If the impact of technology on one area of employment is further examined, it can be seen that, in the United Kingdom at least, machines have largely taken over from men in the agricultural sector (Blaxter, 1974). In the 1920s about one million (1m) people were employed in farming, by 1971 this figure had fallen to less than 400,000. At the same time, the number of horses utilized had fallen from about 1.1m in 1910 to less than 100,000 in 1965. The number of powered machines in use rose considerably over the same period however. For instance, from 1946 to 1971 the number of combine harvesters increased from 3,500 to 66,000, the number of grain driers from 1,000 to 63,500 and the number of tractors from almost 200,000 to well over 400,000. As Blaxter points

13

out, the fuel energy input to British agriculture rose from just over 200m therms in 1938 to around 800m therms in 1970. But, over the period from 1940 to 1970, agricultural output has almost trebled.

Although agriculture is one of the most dramatic examples, changes have also taken place in other areas of employment and several overlapping trends can be discerned. There has been a gradual but accelerating shift from manual to non-manual work and, accompanying this, a shift from unskilled to skilled and professional employment. These changes have meant that the period of time required to be spent in training has tended to rise, but there has also been an increase in the rate at which skills, which previously would have been expected to survive a working lifetime, have become obsolescent. It appears that this 'skill obsolescence' is beginning to affect the rapidly growing 'knowledge industries' (Dubin, 1971). Thus many individuals retiring in the 1970s, who started work presumably some time during the 1920s, will have experienced a number of changes in their working lives. Many workers will have found their skills to have become obsolescent, and will have sought retraining in newer and more marketable skills; others will have found that their expertise will have needed up-dating; others still will have found themselves unemployed and forced to seek a new occupation entirely.

In virtually all societies over the past two centuries the death rate has declined markedly, as a result of advances in medicine, nutrition and public health. This has been followed, some years later, by a decline in the birth rate. The phenomenon has been referred to as the 'demographic transition' and is generally thought to be a concomitant of modernization. It began in the industrialized countries over 200 years ago, whereas most 'underdeveloped' countries are only experiencing it in the present century. During the transition, population rapidly increases because of the lag between the fall in death rates and that in birth rates. The rapid rate of population increase in underdeveloped countries is the main contributor to the population problem the world now faces, although in industrialized countries too populations have been steadily increasing. This has had two main consequences. First, the size of the labour force in most industrialized countries has increased (in Britain by about 35 per cent since the First World War). Given the commitment to full employment that has existed in recent years, this increase in the size of the working population has necessitated the creation of new jobs and/or the expansion of existing ones. Second, the age structure of the population has altered, due to increases in longevity, and dependency ratios have changed. Apart from increases in the number of children of school age, the number of men and women of retirement age has risen. For example, in the United Kingdom, the number of men over 65 and the number of women over 60 per thousand of the population of working age (15 to 59 or 64) rose from 102 in 1901 to 275 in 1972 (*Social Trends*, 1973). The working population has therefore had to support an increasing proportion of the population who are no longer working, although this proportion is likely to stabilize over the next two decades.

In 1901 there were about 5m men between the ages of 15 and 29 and only about 2m between the ages of 45 and 59 in the population of the United Kingdom. By 1970 these totals were 6m (an increase of 20 per cent) and 5m (an increase of 150 per cent) respectively. This demographic change has upset the traditional career pyramid in many occupations and has exerted increasing pressure upon older workers, who tend to have higher than average rates of long-term unemployment. Further discussion of this topic is deferred to Chapter 7.

Changing conceptions of man at work

An individual's orientation to work is not part of his genetic endowment; attitudes toward work and by far the greater part of behaviour in the work situation are socially and culturally determined. People are gradually instructed as to what they may expect and want from work by a variety of socializing agencies, among them the home, the school, the local community and the mass media.

Attitudes to work vary considerably across different cultures and, historically, have undergone a number of transformations. According to Tilgher (1962), 'to the Greeks work was a curse and nothing else', a view which was apparently shared by the Romans and the Hebrews. The early Christians followed the Jewish tradition in considering work to be a punishment for man's original sin. However, they also attributed some positive functions to work, since it provided a means of helping the poor and the needy. Furthermore, work began to be regarded as important both for physical and mental health, since without it men would fall victim to idleness and other, possibly more dangerous, forms of wickedness. These views of work were further developed by Luther, although he expressed them rather more forcefully, concluding that all who could work should, work being not only the universal base of society but also the best way of serving God. Calvin elaborated this doctrine considerably. For him, work was a religious duty and austerity a cardinal virtue. Men must work hard but at the same time they must not enjoy the fruits of their labours.

The doctrines advanced by Luther and Calvin are generally considered to express values and contain ideas which, as the 'Protestant ethic', form the ideological basis of modern capitalism. In the nineteenth century, however, the ascetic component of the Protestant ethic was much reduced and greater emphasis was placed on the material rewards of work. Work thus came to be regarded as a means of individual advancement, offering virtually unlimited opportunities for 'self help' and 'self improvement'.

The gradual introduction of mass production methods (beginning with James Watt's Soho foundry in the 1790s) stemming from the Industrial Revolution in the late eighteenth and early nineteenth centuries, brought about both a complex division of labour and a fragmentation of the work process. This development effectively ousted the small-scale craftsman. It was considered by many social theorists, ranging from Karl Marx to William Morris, to destroy any intrinsic value work might have, since they regarded the individual worker as becoming merely the passive appendage of a machine. The development of time and motion study methods, the devising of payment and production control systems and the promulgation of 'scientific management' by Frederick Winslow Taylor and Frank and Lillian Gilbreth at the end of the last and in the early years of the present century (see E6) probably served to reinforce the views of those who held that work had be-

16

come 'dehumanized', since the declared aim of such methods was to increase productivity and efficiency as much as possible and other considerations were largely ignored. And indeed the techniques pioneered by Taylor and the Gilbreths were largely successful in achieving this aim. However, scientific management also set out to benefit the worker. Taylor's view was that the prosperity of the individual worker was inexorably linked to the success of the firm for which he worked. Thus techniques which increased the efficiency of the firm would also make it more successful, thereby increasing the wellbeing of the labour force and reducing the chances of conflict between management and workers. Taylor's principal goal was to end management by *ad hoc* principles and to put it firmly on a scientific basis. This he saw as being in everyone's interest, believing as he did in 'rational economic man'.

But 'Taylorism' assumed that workers should be studied as isolated units. It argued that the main factors affecting their efficiency were either fatigue, or sub-standard environmental conditions or incorrect methods of carrying out the job which could be remedied by time and motion study methods. Such a view completely neglects other equally important influences on work behaviour emanating from the social environment. This became abundantly clear in the 1920s and '30s when the results of an extensive series of studies carried out at the Hawthorne Electric Company by Elton Mayo and his associates were made available (Roethlisberger and Dickson, 1939). On the basis of these and other related studies, Mayo and others launched what became known as the 'human relations' school.

These studies called attention to the importance of social factors in the work situation. They emphasized the effects of the informal organization of work groups, and the patterns of social interaction that occurred within them, upon job performance and job satisfaction. One study in this series, the 'Bank Wiring Observation Room' study, provided one of the first detailed accounts of the influence of group norms upon output, particularly upon output restriction. It demonstrated convincingly that, for many workers, social factors could override economic considerations. Although many principles of

17

scientific management remain valid, the view of industrial man that it expressed was dealt a severe blow by the Hawthorne experiments from which it has never really recovered.

In the wake of the Hawthorne studies, a new view of industrial man was put forward, that of 'Social Man' who sought satisfaction mainly through membership of a stable work group and the social rewards thereby generated. The lesson for management implied by this view of industrial man was that the basic unit through which management should attempt to achieve its goals was not the individual, isolated worker but the small, stable work group. This led to the utilization of techniques such as 'participatory management' which, in some cases at least, achieved a fair degree of success. But in the opinion of many later theorists, the view of 'social man' adopted by the human relations school probably overemphasized the importance of 'belongingness' and tended to ignore other human needs which might be equally important determinants of work behaviour. McClelland (1961), for example, has emphasized the importance of 'achievement' needs in his work on achievement motivation (see D2).

The final conception of industrial man to be discussed has been described as 'self-actualizing man' and derives from an approach to motivation initiated by Maslow (1943) and extended to work behaviour by Herzberg. Maslow proposed a hierarchy of goals towards which he suggested that human behaviour was directed. These were physiological needs, safety needs, social needs, self-esteem needs and self-actualization needs. Maslow's approach stressed that human behaviour could be viewed as being controlled by several motives but, more importantly, that people often engage in activities which are intrinsically rewarding or satisfying. Work may be one such activity, for some individuals at least. Although Maslow's approach has been influential, it has not generated much empirical research. Herzberg's approach, in contrast, which is similar to Maslow's in some respects, has generated much research as well as a considerable amount of critical scrutiny.

Herzberg's is a two-factor theory of work behaviour, based on the observation that when people described occasions in the work situation when they felt extremely satisfied, the

18

activities involved appeared to be very different from those described as typical occasions when they felt extremely dissatisfied. Satisfaction appeared to be associated with such factors as responsibility, achievement, recognition and the work itself. These are described by Herzberg as *motivators*. Dissatisfaction on the other hand appeared to be associated with such factors as pay, working conditions and the quality of supervision. These are labelled *hygiene factors*. Herzberg argued that effecting a change in hygiene factors, for example, improving working conditions, would not promote satisfaction with work but would merely prevent dissatisfaction. Improvements in satisfaction and work performance would be brought about only by changes in motivators, which would help the individual fulfil the need to self-actualize. Although Herzberg's original findings have not always been confirmed, and inconsistencies in his approach have frequently been pointed out, his research and writings have been influential.

The conception of industrial man as 'self-actualizing' man has meant that greater importance is attached to the intrinsically motivating features of work than was the case previously. It has been argued, for instance, that the monotonous and repetitive nature of many jobs is primarily responsible for a number of persistent industrial problems such as low job satisfaction, high absenteeism and turnover rates and, less frequently but no less importantly, sabotage. This has resulted in a resurgence of interest in job redesign and, more generally, in the factors influencing such aspects of work behaviour as turnover and absenteeism and in the determinants of job satisfaction.

2
Satisfaction and performance at work

In this chapter, we briefly examine a number of aspects of satisfaction and performance at work and the way in which they are related. These include work satisfaction and its relation to work performance, and some of the factors related to absenteeism, turnover, accidents, and stress at work. We begin by considering work satisfaction.

Work satisfaction

An increasing concern with the meaning of work, and the belief that the degree of satisfaction at work is related to aspects of work behaviour such as productivity and to absenteeism and turnover rates, have prompted the growth of a vast research literature (according to some authorities upwards of 4,000 items) on job satisfaction. Nevertheless, as Hinrichs (1968) points out, a clear and widely accepted definition of job satisfaction is still lacking and the concept is in many ways analogous to 'the often used but essentially undefined concept of morale'. Some approaches to job satisfaction, based on statistical factorial analyses of survey data, have suggested that a general factor of job satisfaction exists, although this view has been criticized by Vroom (1964). Others have emphasized a number of specific factors, each related to different aspects of the work situation such as pay, the quality of supervision, opportunities for promotion, status and job content. Herzberg's approach, using the critical incident technique (see p. 100), has suggested that satisfaction and dissatisfaction are not two opposite extremes of the same continuum but are separate dimensions, influenced by different factors in the work situation. Extrinsic or hygiene factors such as pay, working conditions and the quality of supervision affect dissatisfaction, while intrinsic or motivating factors, relating primarily to job content, influence satisfaction. One weakness of this approach, which has been frequently pointed out, is that the dichotomous nature of satisfaction may in fact result from the research technique employed. Kahn (1972) has suggested that the question of work satisfaction is too closely interwoven with that of personal identity and self-esteem to be answered simply, since the choice for most workers is a work connection 'burdened with negative qualities' or no work connection at all. Thus when asked whether they are satisfied with their work situation, most workers have no difficulty in responding affirmatively. A recent survey of job satisfaction in Britain found that 87 per cent of men, and 91.8 per cent of women, reported themselves as either 'very satisfied' or 'fairly satisfied' with their jobs (*Social Trends*, 1973).

Several methods of assessing job satisfaction have been developed, usually employing attitude questionnaire or interview techniques. The various methods of attitude scale construction will not be discussed in any detail here; a useful summary is provided by Edwards (1957). Suffice it to say that of the three main methods, those of Guttman, Thurstone and Likert, the last is generally assumed to have somewhat higher reliability, as well as being less time consuming to construct and to administer. A number of questionnaires have been developed which measure job attitudes on a number of dimensions. One of the best known of these is the Job Descriptive Index (Smith, Kendall and Hulin, 1969) which, on the basis of factor analyses of job satisfaction dimensions, assesses satisfaction in five areas: (1) work (2) pay (3) promotion opportunities (4) supervision and (5) fellow workers.

As will be seen in Ch. 4, the interview has been widely used in selection procedures, despite the fact that a number of studies have suggested that it is an inefficient technique. With respect to attempts to predict job attitudes on the basis of interviews, much the same conclusions can be drawn. Even when the results obtained from interviews prove to be reliable, the interview is manifestly not tapping the same processes as the questionnaire. One way in which the interview method has been used in attempts to assess job satisfaction is the 'leaving' or 'exit' interview, involving individuals who are voluntarily terminating employment and who may, therefore, tend to be more frank about the advantages and disadvantages of the job. However, in general, there is little agreement between the results obtained by this procedure and those obtained by questionnaire. Often either pay or promotion is given as the reason for leaving and this tends to preclude discussion about other possible reasons for termination.

A number of attitudes both of the individual and of the work situation have been studied in relation to job satisfaction although only a selection of these will be considered here. In spite of the fact that both in the United States and in Britain women tend for the most part to work in less skilled jobs, to have lower occupational status and to receive lower rates of pay, a number of studies have reported that women are generally more satisfied with their work than men. However, the fact that similar results are reported in situations where men and women are engaged on the same jobs, have the same status and receive the same pay has suggested that these factors may not contribute as much to the job satisfaction of women as they appear to do for men; for women job satisfaction may depend more on other factors, such as the social aspects of work (Myers, 1964).

Job satisfaction appears to increase with age, although most of these studies have been cross-sectional ones in which groups of workers, each group consisting of a different age-range, have been compared. The difficulty with this method is that the groups were not only of different ages but also of different generations. However, the sample used in one of the first studies of job satisfaction (Hoppock, 1935) was followed up twenty-seven years later. In other words, the same people were interviewed at different ages. This is one of the few longitudinal studies in the area of age and job satisfaction.

Although his sample was a small one, Hoppock found that out of the 23 cases investigated, for 17 people job satisfaction had increased and decreased for only two.

Age is usually confounded (see A8) with length of service (although the two are not perfectly related) and hence often with changes in the kind of work performed. Herzberg, Mausner, Peterson and Capwell (1957), in their review of research on job attitudes, suggested that a U-shaped function described the relation both between age and satisfaction and between satisfaction and length of service. Hulin and Smith (1965), however, argued that there was a linear relationship between satisfaction and both variables. Saleh and Otis (1964) suggested that the relation between satisfaction and age increased until shortly before retirement, when it declined quite sharply, although the methodology of this study has been criticised, since it employed a retrospective technique. When length of service is carefully controlled for, there appears to be a linear increase in job satisfaction with age but a slight *decline* with time in the job (Gibson and Klein, 1971).

As might be expected, a negative relationship has usually been found between neuroticism and job satisfaction. The dissatisfied worker has been portrayed as less able to form relationships with others, as having more neurotic symptoms and poorer personal adjustment and as being less extraverted.

Job satisfaction tends to increase with job level in the organizational hierarchy. Thus supervisors tend to have higher satisfaction than workers and the higher the management position the greater the job satisfaction. In general, too, line managers are more satisfied than staff managers (Porter and Lawler, 1965). More generally, individuals working in small groups tend to be more satisfied than those working in large groups.

There are also large differences in job satisfaction across occupations. In one survey it was found that an average of 43 per cent of white collar workers, but only 24 per cent of blue collar workers, would choose similar work again (O'Toole, 1973).

Occupational differences in job satisfaction are sometimes thought to reflect differences in job content, particularly in the degree of autonomy, responsibility and flexibility that different occupations provide. These job content factors are generally considered to be among the major determinants of job satisfaction. The prestige of an occupation also appears to influence job satisfaction, high prestige occupations being associated with greater satisfaction than low prestige ones.

Job performance

The measurement of the job performance of different groups of workers is clearly a complex operation. Firstly it has to be decided what groups are to be compared. In order to make reliable comparisons the effects of experience and type of work have to be controlled for and some attempt made to ensure that the groups being compared are using similar equipment and working in much the same conditions. Clearly such conditions are rarely met in practice although a number of apparently well controlled studies of performance comparisons among factory and office workers have been reported.

Secondly, a choice of performance measure has to be made. Several are available, including job proficiency tests, job samples, behaviour check lists, output measures based on production records and supervisory and merit ratings. A detailed summary of such performance appraisal techniques is provided by Bass and Barrett (1972).

Performance and job satisfaction

There have been frequent attempts to demonstrate that satisfaction and job performance are positively related in order that attempts to increase job satisfaction could be shown to have practical consequences. However, the main conclusion of one of the first comprehensive reviews of the relation between satisfaction and performance (Brayfield and Crockett, 1955) was that there was little convincing evidence of any strong relationship between the two. Similarly, Vroom (1964) found evidence of only a low positive relationship (a median correlation of + .14) between satisfaction and performance in the studies he surveyed. Since performance and satisfaction appear to be only tangentially related, it seems likely that programmes designed to increase satisfacton at work are unlikely to exert much effect upon job performance.

This could be for a variety of reasons. Firstly, in many work situations, job performance cannot vary very much; either, for example, because the way the work flow is arranged does not permit it or, perhaps, because output is restricted by prevailing 'group norms'. Secondly, there are large individual differences in motivation among workers (Hackman, 1969). Some are presumably highly satisfied with jobs in which demands on performance are slight while others are best satisfied when great demands are made on their performance capacity. It would also be expected that the degree of fit between an individual's abilities and skills and the requirements of the job he is doing would influence the relationship between satisfaction and performance (Lawler, 1966). If the fit is a poor one, the relation between satisfaction and performance is likely to be low, or there may be no relationship at all. If, on the other hand, there is a good match between abilities and job requirements then there might well be a high positive relationship between the two variables. These expectations were confirmed by Carlson (1969), using a sample of 500 workers.

An alternative way of considering the possible relation between performance and satisfaction is to regard job satisfaction as being likely to *result* from performance at the job, rather than being a potential determinant of it. Thus, job satisfaction would be increased when the individual believes he is obtaining rewards from the work situation through his own efforts. However, Porter and Lawler (1968a) point out that the majority of studies of the relation between satisfaction and performance have been carried out at the 'rank and file level of organizations' where little flexibility of performance is possible and where the rewards workers obtain are determined by factors largely beyond their control. Thus little relation between satisfaction and performance would be expected. However, studies of the relation between these two variables in managers and executives, for whom both rewards and performance can show much greater concomitant variation, have not consistently produced as high correlations as might be expected.

Satisfaction and performance therefore do not seem to be strongly related, although, as mentioned above, one reason for this may be limitations imposed on possible performance variation. Other ways in which behaviour can vary, and in which dissatisfaction with work may be expressed, are to be absent from work or to leave the work situation altogether. As will be seen below, the relation between absenteeism and turnover measures and satisfaction with work appear to be much more clear cut.

Absenteeism and turnover

The health status of the working population clearly bears an important relationship to its potential productivity, and in terms of the majority of indices the populations of most industrialized countries are becoming healthier. However, at the same time, sickness absence rates are rising, particularly in terms of frequency. Taylor (1968) indicates that the mean rate of increase in sickness absence frequency in a number of European countries, including Britain, over the period 1950–68 was 34 per cent, whereas the rate of increase in severity (the length of a given spell of absence) was only 19 per cent. Furthermore, the total number of working days lost annually through sickness absence is vastly higher than the number lost through industrial stoppages. In Britain in 1967, for example, 301m working days were lost through certified sickness compared to just under 3m for industrial stoppages (Semmence, 1971). These figures also take no account of uncertified absences or those due to industrial injuries. It is not surprising therefore that the cost of absenteeism is enormous. As Semmence observes, 'The cost to the National Insurance fund in 1966–67 of £261.8 million was only a fraction of the cost to the community in lost production, estimated at £1,200 million, and of the cost borne by many firms in retaining an extra 5 per cent of employees to cover sickness absence'.

Absenteeism is sometimes considered to be one extreme of a continuum of 'withdrawal behaviour' progressing, at the other extreme, to the decision to leave the job (Herzberg, Mausner, Peterson and Capwell, 1957). A second view is adopted by Hill and Trist (1955), who regard absences and accidents as one kind of withdrawal behaviour, and turnover as another. A third view is that absenteeism and turnover, whether related or not, have common underlying causes. Thus three questions arise: (1) Are absenteeism and turnover related? (2) Are absenteeism rates predictive of subsequent turnover? and (3) Are the two kinds of behaviour determined by the same factors? Both Lyons (1972) and Porter and Speers (1973) have provided comprehensive reviews of research pertinent to these questions.

The first question can be considered in the light of results obtained with individuals and with groups. At the individual level it is clear that absenteeism and turnover are significantly related, that is, those who are more often absent from work are more likely to leave their job. At the group level the evidence is more ambiguous, although the same conclusion appears to be warranted. With respect to the second question, Lyons (1972) suggests that the available evidence supports the view of a progressive continuum of withdrawal behaviour, beginning with absenteeism and ending with turnover. However, with respect to the third, there appears to be little support for the hypothesis that the two kinds of behaviour have the same determinants, although they may well share some common correlates. Porter and Speers (1973) point out that there are a number of respects in which absenteeism can be distinguished from turnover as a form of withdrawal behaviour. First, the consequences of absenteeism are much less severe, at least for the individual. Second, the decision to be absent from a job is much easier to make than the decision to leave it altogether. Third, the decision to leave may well depend on whether alternative opportunities for employment are available. If they are not then absenteeism may sometimes become a substitute for terminating employment. Some of the characteristics of the individual and factors in the work setting are now briefly surveyed in terms of their relationship to absenteeism and turnover.

Women take more certified sickness absence, age for age, than do men, and married women have more certified absence than single women at all ages. Women also tend to have higher turnover rates. As far as age is concerned, in terms of the duration of absence, absenteeism rises with age, but in terms of frequency it declines. Taylor (1967) found that the frequency for men aged 50–59 was only half that of men aged 20–29 but the duration was twice as long. Turnover rates, too, generally decline with age. As already noted, age and length of service tend to be closely linked, and longitudinal studies of absenteeism and turnover are comparatively rare. However, in one such study, carried out by Hill and Trist (1955), absenteeism and length of service were found to be unrelated. With respect to turnover, a number of studies have reported the length of service of employees in their previous jobs to be a good predictor of length of service in the current job.

In an examination of the personality correlates of sickness absence, Taylor (1969) found that the 'never sick' were characterized by high introversion and low neuroticism (see D3), the 'frequently sick' by high extraversion and the 'long sick' by high neuroticism. Manifest anxiety has also been found to be a correlate of absenteeism among industrial workers, the greater the anxiety the higher the rate of absenteeism. Personality differences have also been found to be related to turnover, leavers in general having different characteristics from stayers. The former, at least among technical and scientific personnel, have been found to possess higher levels of achievement, independence and aggression, while the latter appear to be more emotionally stable and mature.

Turning to factors in the work situation, the quality or style of supervision appears to be a major factor in determining turnover, although its relation to absenteeism has not been studied (Porter and Speers, 1973). The size of the work unit also appears to affect turnover, at least in industrial workers. In general, the greater the size, the higher the turnover rate. Absenteeism rates also tend to increase as the work unit becomes larger. One study (Ingham, 1970) also found absenteeism to be significantly and positively related to the size of firm, although turnover rates were not. Dissatisfaction with job content factors, in particular task repetitiveness, has been shown to relate positively to turnover rates in both industrial and clerical workers. Absenteeism appears to show similar trends. Finally, job level and the degree of perceived autonomy and responsibility are also strongly and positively associated with both absenteeism and turnover. Howell (1968), for example, found that the absence rates of secretaries, who were assumed to have greater autonomy and responsibility, were about 60 per cent of those for women clerical officers, despite the fact that both groups had similar social and educational backgrounds and received similar rates of pay.

However, although many of these factors are of considerable importance, it is clear that job satisfaction is probably one of the major determinants of the two kinds of withdrawal behaviour that have been considered, as is emphasized by Taylor (1969) and Porter and Speers (1973). With respect to sickness absence, Taylor observes that 'job satisfaction is one of the most important causative factors'. With respect to turnover Porter and Speers indicate that, 'In general, very strong evidence has been found in support of the contention that *overall* job satisfaction represents an important force in the individual's participation decision' (their italics), although they suggest that the evidence is less definite for absenteeism. Of the fifteen studies reviewed by Porter and Speers, all except one found a negative relationship between turnover and job satisfaction (i.e. the lower the turnover, the higher the job satisfaction and vice-versa) and both of those concerned with absenteeism obtained similar findings. Earlier research reviewed by Brayfield and Crockett (1955) and Vroom (1964), although often methodologically less rigorous and using weaker job satisfaction measures than later studies, suggests the same conclusion concerning the importance of job satisfaction.

Porter and Speers interpret these findings with respect to turnover in terms of 'expectancy theory' (see Ch. 6) and suggest that this theory can probably accommodate the absenteeism data as well. As noted earlier, job satisfaction can be considered to depend on rewards obtained in the work situation. Furthermore, when an individual enters the work situation for the first time he has certain expectations about the kinds of rewards he will receive, and places different values upon them. Porter and Speers argue that if these expectations concerning rewards, particularly those that are highly valued, are not met then job satisfaction decreases and withdrawal behaviour may occur. However, the critical level, or threshold, that has to be reached for absenteeism is lower than that for turnover, since it represents a less drastic form of withdrawal.

It seems clear then that job satisfaction is closely linked to turnover and absenteeism. We turn next to a brief consideration of accidents.

Accidents

Accidents have also been regarded as a form of withdrawal behaviour. Hill and Trist (1953, 1955) studied both absenteeism and accident rates in a steel works and found that the number of unsanctioned absences declined with length of service, as did accident rates, but the number of sanctioned absences, which included certified absences, tended to increase. They suggested that, given the nature of the work, workers believed that a certain level of absenteeism was legitimate, but strong social pressures operated as to the form in which this should be taken. Certified absence and certain other sanctioned absences were permissible, but uncertified absences and those due to accidents were not. However, they did find that 'accident repeaters' tended to have a far larger number of unsanctioned absences than workers who had no accidents. Accident repeaters thus appeared to be workers who did not accept the prevailing 'group norms', and accidents could therefore be regarded as a form of withdrawal from the work situation. However, Castle (1956), who attempted to replicate Hill and Trist's findings in a photographic process plant, failed to do so. It thus remains unclear whether or not accidents should be viewed as a further form of withdrawal behaviour and, indeed, few studies have followed up this particular approach.

A variety of definitions of the term 'accident' have been proposed. Arbous and Kerrich (1951) define an accident as 'an unplanned event in a chain of planned or controlled events' and Cherns (1962) as 'an error with sad consequences'. Drew (1963) estimates that between 80 per cent and 90 per cent of accidents are the result of 'human error'. An accident then is an event, resulting from unintended or 'error' be-

30

haviour, which has consequences serious enough to be reported. Hale and Hale (1971) have pointed out that the practical difficulties of collecting data on accidents which do not result in injuries have effectively compelled researchers to concentrate on those that do.

Unlike sickness absence, the number of working days lost through industrial injuries has remained at a fairly stable level over the past few years. In 1960–1, 17m working days were lost in British industry for this reason, while in 1971–2 this figure was 16m, although slightly higher figures obtained in some intervening years. In terms of the number of deaths resulting from accidents, the figures for transport accidents, running at an annual rate of about 7500, are far in excess of those for industrial accidents, where the annual rate is just over 1000. In 1971 the manufacturing industries accounted for about one quarter of this total.

Accident research has considered both personal and situational factors in the causation of accidents, although the former have received greater emphasis. Probably one of the best known hypotheses concerning the causation of accidents is the notion of 'accident proneness', stemming from some of the earliest work on industrial accidents carried out by the Industrial Fatigue Research Board in Britain during the First World War (Greenwood and Woods, 1919). These researchers set up three hypotheses concerning the distribution of accidents in a population exposed to equal risk – first, that the distribution was purely random; second, that having had one accident altered the probability of having a second, either increasing or decreasing it; and third, that some individuals are initially more likely to have accidents than others. The latter became known as the 'accident proneness' hypothesis. It was further argued that, given certain assumptions, these three hypotheses could be portrayed by different statistical distributions which could be fitted to observed accident data. In a number of careful studies, evidence emerged which appeared to support the accident proneness hypothesis, although this evidence was cautiously interpreted. Nevertheless, some individuals seemed to be 'accident prone' and accident proneness gradually became regarded as a stable characteristic of the individual. In the 1940s and the 1950s the concept of 'accident proneness' began to come under attack on both theoretical and empirical grounds. Arbous and Kerrich (1951) argued that in the original Industrial Fatigue Research Board experiments, insufficient care had been taken to ensure that members of the populations selected for study were at equal risk and that in addition, the assumptions relating the original hypotheses to the expected statistical distributions of accident data were not sufficiently rigorous. Adelstein (1952), in a study of accident rates in railway shunters, obtained data supporting the 'random hypothesis', at least in individuals with up to five years service, although the accident proneness hypothesis tended to be slightly better supported after a longer period in the job. This finding cast some doubt on the view that accident proneness was a stable individual characteristic.

Subsequently, although the concept of accident proneness has continued to receive criticism, it has also had some support. Currently, the concept seems to be viewed with a cautious neutrality. In one recent review of accident research, Kay (1971) has argued that although the accident proneness hypothesis should be regarded as 'unproven', it should not be 'summarily rejected'.

Finally, the relation between job satisfaction and accidents is briefly considered. Kerr (1950) suggested, largely on the basis of his own research, that just under half of the variation in accident rates between individuals was related to dissatisfaction with work, about half to the stresses of the job, and the remainder to individual characteristics or accident proneness. Most studies which have examined the relation between satisfaction and accidents have not been able to equate the degree of risk to which individuals are subjected. One study which controlled for this factor, as well as a number of other variables, found a highly significant relationship between the number of accidents and the degree of dissatisfaction with work (Davids and Mahoney, 1957). Hale and Hale (1971) point out that few conclusions can be drawn from the bulk of research in this area because of poor methodology and conclude that it cannot be stated 'with any certainty' that increasing job satisfaction will reduce accidents. However, the question of whether the reduction of accidents through, for example, increased safety measures increases job satisfaction seems not to have been investigated.

Stress at work

The term 'stress' is often thought to be over-used and under-defined, yet it is one which many people seem to understand readily. It is used here to refer to the effects aspects of the work situation may exert on physical and mental health, specifically the so-called 'stress diseases', such as coronary heart disease, and symptoms of mental illness (see F3).

In Britain, the United States and many European countries, about half the deaths each year, for both men and women, are due to cardiovascular diseases. The factors associated with a high risk of heart disease include cigarette smoking, high blood pressure, cholesterol and blood sugar levels, and excess body weight. However, a number of studies have indicated that social and psychological factors may account for much of the risk (see, for example, French and Caplan, 1970) and this has prompted research into factors in the work situation that may increase susceptibility to heart disease. Among the factors that have been shown to influence such susceptibility are dissatisfaction with work (Sales and House, 1971) and occupational stress.

Components of occupational stress have been taken to include responsibility, particularly for other people, exceptionally heavy workloads and status incongruence (a situation where an individual's job level is not matched by other variables such as his educational level). All these factors have been shown to exert some influence on susceptibility to heart disease. Furthermore, certain personality characteristics, such as 'excessive drive, aggressiveness, ambition, involvement in competitive activities, frequent vocational deadlines, pressure for vocational productivity and an enhanced sense of time urgency' have been held to distinguish coronary-prone individuals from those with low coronary risk, who are more relaxed and easy-going, rarely become impatient and spend more time in leisure pursuits (Jenkins, Rosenman and Friedman, 1967).

Stress is frequently considered to be an occupational hazard

33

of managers and executives, and some research supports this view. However, in one of the major studies in this area – a large scale investigation of the incidence of coronary heart disease among managers and workers employed by the Bell System Operating Companies in the United States – this was not found to be the case (Hinkle *et al* 1968). Every disability and death due to coronary heart disease over a three-year period (1963–6) was recorded from a population of 270,000 employees. The number of such incidents was over 6000. These data were then related to educational level, job level, length of time in present job and two measures of career mobility, the different number of jobs held within the company and the number of companies within the Bell System in which the individual had worked. The results showed that managers and executives experienced fewer coronary incidents than did foremen and workers. In addition, Hinkle *et al* found no relationship between career mobility and job success and the incidence of heart disease. They concluded that their findings provided no evidence 'that men who have high levels of responsibility, or who have been promoted rapidly, frequently or recently, or men who are transferred to new departments or to new companies, have any added risk of coronary heart disease'. Furthermore, it was found that men who entered the company with a college degree experienced fewer coronary incidents at all ages, in all geographical areas and in all departments of the organization than those who did not. Hinkle *et al* interpreted these differences in coronary attack rate related to educational level in terms of the probably better biological make-up of the more highly educated group, which was thought to be 'related to, but not necessarily the result of, differences in the social and economic background from which they originated'.

From this study, it appears that managers and executives are somewhat less likely to experience attacks of coronary heart disease than are workers, although this finding should be treated with caution. It has also been shown that managers report themselves as less anxious and apprehensive than do production workers (Hackman, 1969). The latter group also perceived themselves as more aggressive and less industrious. Hackman developed a series of self-description scales based on existing tests and surveyed over 1000 individuals in different job groupings in terms of the way in which they perceived themselves and their behaviour at work. Scores on these self-description scales were also related to job proficiency. Although there were differences between different job groups with respect to the relation between job proficiency and scores on particular self-description scales, in almost all job groups anxiety was negatively related to proficiency. As noted above, high anxiety was more frequently reported by production workers.

Probably the factors affecting feelings of anxiety and symptoms of stress among industrial workers, including job security, potential job hazards and the pace of the job, are different from those affecting mental health, although there may be some overlap between them.

According to one of the best known studies of mental health in industry (Kornhauser, 1965) mental health is liable to be impaired by the low self-esteem and feelings of frustration and powerlessness engendered by many low-level industrial jobs. Kornhauser's study was carried out on a sample of 407 car assembly workers in Detroit in the early 1950s and, according to a recent report on *Work in America* (O'Toole, 1973), it is generally regarded today as being an 'underestimate of the mental health problems of automobile (assembly-line) workers, especially with respect to the alienation of young workers'.

Kornhauser's study was meticulously carried out and his main conclusions are clear. Some 40 per cent of workers showed symptoms of mental ill-health problems. Furthermore, mental health was positively and significantly related to job satisfaction and both these variables were positively related to self-esteem and to the skill level of the jobs held. Pay and conditions of work were much less accurate predictors of mental health than job content factors, such as the challenge and interest of the job.

Kornhauser's definition of mental health was a broad one. It emphasized positive mental health and was not concerned with psychiatric diagnostic categories. Kornhauser states that by 'positive mental health' he meant a 'personal condition that expresses itself in a response of greater self-esteem, morale

35

and trust in people, friendly inter-personal relations, relative satisfaction with life, emotional security and freedom from interfering manifestations of anxiety'. Other studies which have used diagnostic categories, for example Fraser (1947), have arrived at many of the same conclusions as Kornhauser, in particular with respect to neurotic disorders. Fraser's study of engineering workers (virtually the only large-scale British study to have examined mental health in industry) does suffer from some methodological weaknesses particularly with respect to data analysis, and so the conclusions should be treated with caution. But it is a well-controlled study in many respects. Fraser found that a number of job content factors appeared to be associated with the development of neurosis in workers whose health records had previously been good. Monotony and boredom, close attention to detail, and light and sedentary work were factors which appeared to be important in this respect.

The broad conclusion from this chapter is that job content factors are of great importance in influencing job satisfaction which in turn is strongly related to many aspects of work behaviour, including the worker's mental health. Not surprisingly, therefore, attempts have been made to increase job satisfaction through work design, and some of these are described in the following chapter.

3
Work design

Introduction

As noted in Chapter 1, technological advances have contributed to productivity increases in a number of fields over
the past few decades. For example, in the United States in
1947 it required 310 man hours to manufacture a motor car,
whereas in 1962 only 153 man hours were needed. The
change over the same period in coal-mining was even more
marked. In 1947, 1300 man hours were required to produce
1000 tons of coal. By 1962, this figure had fallen to 500 man
hours (Bass and Barrett, 1972). Such productivity increases
generally necessitate radical transformations of the way in
which work is carried out. The appropriate design of jobs and
the working environment to accommodate technological in-
novations and at the same time maintain or even improve
worker satisfaction, can thus be seen to be of considerable
importance.

Over the years, three main approaches to work design have
gradually evolved, emphasizing respectively job rationalization, job content and the work role (Davis, 1972). The former
approach attempts to promote more effective work performance, while the latter two are much more concerned with
raising worker satisfaction. Although its historic roots can
probably be traced back further, the development of the job

rationalization approach in the present century begins with the 'scientific management' school of F. W. Taylor and the Gilbreths, whose conception of industrial man as 'rational economic man' was described in Chapter 1. Later in the 1940s and 1950s, the emerging disciplines of human engineering and ergonomics began to apply the methods and techniques of anatomy, physiology and experimental psychology to the design of jobs and of the working environment. Subsequently with the development of more advanced industrial and military systems, there has been a greater emphasis on 'systems ergonomics'. More recently, systems psychologists have been increasingly concerned with the reduction of human error in man-machine systems (Singleton, 1971).

In many instances, one of the major consequences of job rationalization has been that jobs have been broken down into a smaller number of tasks, each involving a smaller number of operations. Furthermore the same tasks are carried out repeatedly and the amount of time taken to perform them is reduced. An example is the car assembly line (see p. 53) where the requirements of the assembly line can seriously reduce job satisfaction. Attempts have been made to enlarge the content of assembly line jobs in order to increase satisfaction, promote better job performance, and reduce absenteeism and turnover, by giving workers a larger number of operations to carry out at the same level in the organizational hierarchy. This procedure is known as *horizontal job enlargement*. More recently, as noted in Chapter 1, Herzberg has also emphasized the importance of intrinsic features of the jobs for the satisfaction of the worker. This has generated interest in *vertical job enlargement*, also known as job enrichment, in which the responsibility of workers is increased by involving them in some supervisory functions. As will be seen below (p. 54), a number of studies of the effectiveness of job enlargement have been carried out, although the results have been suggestive rather than conclusive.

The third approach to work design examines in what ways the technological features of a particular production process affect the social relationships formed in the work situation. Woodward (1958), whose work on management control systems is outlined in Chapter 7, has categorized industrial technology in terms of three kinds of production systems, unit production, mass production and process production. She has also described the different social groupings which tend to evolve in each type of system. Similarly, Sayles (1958) has suggested that different kinds of group behaviour are characteristic of different technologies and concludes that the social relationship between workers dictated by the flow of work is one of the most important variables determining the internal social system of the work group. This approach to work design thus emphasizes the 'socio-technical system' in which the man-machine system is embedded.

In the remainder of this chapter we shall consider in more detail the contributions of these three approaches to work design, beginning with ergonomics.

Ergonomics and work design

Ergonomics is an inter-disciplinary approach to the problem of fitting the task to the man. The disciplines involved are: anatomy, physiology and psychology. Anatomical data are applied, for instance, to the design of seating and the layout of work places. Physiological data on bodily processes can be used to calculate tolerance limits for given physical work loads or for exposure to adverse environmental conditions such as high temperatures. Since in most advanced industrial systems man acts primarily as an information processor, or a monitor or a decision maker, the application of psychological methods, in laboratory and field studies, enables these functions to be better understood and the inherent limitations on human performance to be circumvented or minimized.

One of the first ergonomic decisions to be made in work system design concerns the allocation of function between man and machine (see E4). This is determined both by their relative capabilities and the relative economic costs involved. There are clearly a number of ways in which machines are superior to men, for example in terms of speed, power and consistency of operation. Men are superior to machines, for example, in flexibility and the ability to make decisions under conditions of uncertainty. Nevertheless, since economic considerations are of equal, if not greater, importance when compared to ergonomic ones, allocation of function inevitably becomes a 'trade-off' between the two.

Once the responsibilities of the human operator within the system have been defined, the various tasks he must carry out have to be designed so that he works in as close harmony as possible with the rest of the system. In order for a man-machine system to be effective, the man and the machine must exchange information. The machine sends information to the man via a *display*, which enables him to monitor its progress and to know when to take action himself. Displays are of three main types, qualitative (e.g. a warning light), quantitative (e.g. a linear scale or a counter) and representational, which provides the operator with a 'working model' of the process he is monitoring. After a decision has been taken about what action is required on the basis of information provided by the display, the operator must convey this decision to the rest of the system in the most efficient way possible. This is achieved by a *control*, such as a switch, a crank or a foot pedal. The changed state of the display then provides feedback to the operator as to whether the action taken was appropriate, although information of this kind is also provided by the 'feel' of the control. The *'display-control loop'* is thus the basic element of a man-machine system.

An enormous amount of work has been conducted on the optimal design of displays and controls in order that they may conform as closely as possible with human capabilities for receiving and transmitting information (Murrell, 1965), and it is only possible to summarize some of the main points here.

Displays

In designing displays, the following considerations should be taken into account: (1) The normal and maximal distances at which the display will be read; (2) How quickly display information must be transmitted to the operator; (3) How accurately this information must be transmitted; (4) The amount of information about the process being monitored that the display must convey; and (5) The range of equipment error. Once these data are available, decisions can be taken about the most appropriate kind of display for presenting the relevant information.

Qualitative displays are appropriate when the operator is required to distinguish between a small number of possible states of the environment, for instance, open or shut, or on or off, or when he merely needs to know when a variable has reached a critical level. In the latter case, auditory displays such as buzzers or bells can be useful, as well as visual indicators such as warning lights. The main requirement for qualitative displays is that the different states of the environment should be distinctively represented so that they are readily discriminable, for example by differences in colour, shape or size.

Quantitative displays are clearly essential where numerical information is required. Numerical information may be presented using either *analogue* or *digital* indicators. Analogue indicators, such as meters and gauges, are so called because they provide a visual analogue of a numerical value, whereas digital indicators, such as counters, present numerical information directly. These two kinds of indicator possess different advantages and disadvantages. If precise information is required, then it is better to use a digital indicator, although analogue indicators can be read more rapidly, as well as enabling reasonably accurate readings to be obtained when necessary and thus provide more flexibility.

A considerable amount of research has been conducted on the optimal presentation of scalar information on analogue displays (Singleton, 1969). First, in deciding how a scale should be marked off into divisions, a compromise must be effected between speed and accuracy of reading. The use of too many scale divisions permits greater accuracy but results in loss of speed; if too few are used, reading tends to be rapid but unreliable. To resolve this dilemma, a number of studies of man's ability to make interpolations between scale divisions have been conducted and the general result has been that the best compromise between speed and accuracy is achieved if the scale is divided into four or five subdivisions, although for mechanical scales subdivision into halves is usually recommended. Furthermore, the less cluttered the scale, the easier it will be to read, and for the most part, numbers should be marked only against major scale divisions. In general, the best

41

types of scale for combining accuracy and speed of reading are those indicated in Fig. 3.1.

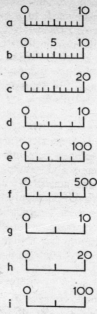

Fig 3.1 *Scale divisions. In general the best type of scale for combined accuracy and speed of reading is (a); the accuracy of reading is only very slightly diminished with (g)*
From *Applied Ergonomics*, March 1970

Second, the size of the subdivisions of the scale should be sufficiently large to be easily discriminated by the operator at normal viewing distances. Factors which are important here are the contrast of scale numbers, scale marks and pointers with the scale background, and the ambient illumination level of the work setting. Much work has also been done on the optimal dimensions of letters, numbers and scale strokes and recommendations can be found in a number of handbooks of equipment design (e.g. Morgan, Cook, Chapanis and Lund, 1963). More generally, some scale shapes are easier to read than others; circular dials tend to be easier than linear scales and when the latter have been evaluated, horizontal scales have been found to be more easily read than vertical. Greater efficiency also results if a pointer moves against a fixed scale, rather than a scale against a fixed pointer, since with minimal experience, estimates of rates of change and check readings of absolute values can be rapidly obtained.

Third, the layout of a scale should take advantage, wherever possible, of expectations and reading habits already established by the operator. For example, scale numbers should increase in a clockwise direction for a circular scale, left to right for a horizontal scale and in an upward direction if a vertical scale is in use.

Representational displays are becoming much more widely used, particularly in large remote control systems in automated plants, since they enable faults or delays in process flow to be detected quickly and accurately. The principal design requirement is that such displays should represent the processes involved as simply and as logically as possible, and design recommendations from work with qualitative and quantitative displays can help materially in this respect.

Finally, in many automated systems, the operator is required to monitor several displays at once. Some of the principles determining the positioning of displays include function, displays with similar functions being grouped together; relative importance, whereby the most important displays are located in optimal viewing positions; and the normal sequence in which they are used.

Controls

There are a number of different types of control used in modern industrial systems and, as with displays, each has its advantages and disadvantages. The main types of controls are horizontal and vertical levers, joy sticks, gear levers, cranks, handwheels, knobs (either with continuous or step functions), press buttons and footpedals.

Controls can be evaluated in terms of the speed and accuracy with which they can be activated, the energy expenditure required to do so and the range of control available. In terms of speed, all the controls mentioned above are efficient, except for large cranks, handwheels and knobs with continuous

43

functions, but, as far as accuracy is concerned, the position is more equivocal. Gear levers, handwheels and knobs are good, the remainder are of moderate or low efficiency. The amount of energy expenditure required is low for foot pedals, joy sticks and large cranks, but moderate to high for the rest. Cranks provide the largest range.

Clearly, the layout of controls should conform as closely as possible to the anatomical dimensions of the human body and to the functions the limbs perform. An example of poor control positioning is shown in Figure 3.2 opposite.

Hand controls should be located within easy reaching distance between elbow and shoulder height and distances between controls should match anatomical considerations. In general, operations requiring speed and precision should be performed by the hands, or fingers, and those requiring force by the feet. As with displays, the movement of controls should conform with previously existing expectations, or 'direction of motion stereotypes' (Loveless, 1962). For example, a machine tool operator expects a cross-slide to move away from him if he turns a handwheel on the front of the machine in a clockwise direction. Warrick (1947) carried out a study on the compatibility of single controls using a panel of lights which lit up in sequence as the control was rotated. He found a very clear pattern of natural relationships to exist when the direction of movement of the control and the direction of illumination of the display were in the same plane. The most natural relationship was one where a clockwise or counter-clockwise movement of the control produces a change in the same direction on the display. When the control and display were not in the same planes, the 'natural' relationship was not so clear-cut however. The conclusions drawn from this and similar studies have been that, where possible, the display should move in the same direction as the control itself. If a knob or a switch, or a lever or a crank, revolves to the right, the pointer on the display should move to the right, or in an upward direction if the display is vertical.

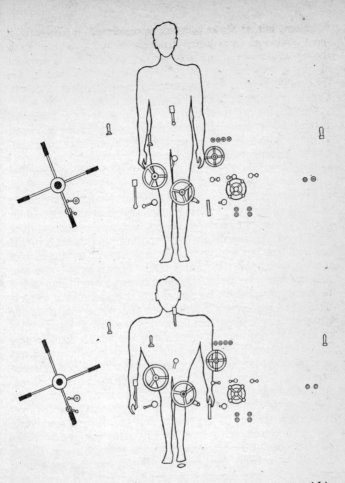

Fig. 3.2 *The controls of a lathe in current use are not within easy reach of the average man, but are so placed that the ideal operator should be 1,372 mm (4½ ft) tall, 610 mm (2 ft) across the shoulders, and have a 2,348 mm (8 ft) arm span*
From *Applied Ergonomics*, December 1969

Some effects of the physical environment on human performance

Besides concerning itself with the design of tasks, ergonomics has also devoted much attention to the effects of the ambient environment on human efficiency and well-being at work. Thus a considerable body of evidence exists concerning the effects of the thermal environment and appropriate criteria for illumination levels and noise exposures. However, here we briefly outline some of the effects of noise upon efficiency, not only because noise is a notable constituent of many industrial settings (Department of Employment, 1971) but also because research on noise and efficiency illustrates the interaction between laboratory and field studies in the understanding of human performance.

Most early industrial studies of the effects of noise on work performance suffered from the 'Hawthorne effect' in that although reducing the level of noise produced an improvement in productivity, so did restoring the noise to its original level. In other words, the introduction into a work situation of any kind of change which employees interpreted as being directed at improving their welfare brought about an improvement in efficiency. Thus, any improvement in efficiency resulting from the reduction of ambient noise levels was not specific to noise but would be produced by any kind of change in working conditions.

At the same time, laboratory studies of noise and efficiency, which did not encounter the difficulties inherent in industrial studies, tended to show no impairment of efficiency that could be attributed to noise, in a wide variety of task situations. Subsequently, it began to be suspected that previous research had relied on tasks which were either not sufficiently sensitive to noise effects, or which lasted for too short a time for these effects to appear. Thus, much research effort was devoted to finding combinations of noise and task variables which would produce impairments of efficiency *attributable* to noise. The kind of noise used was typically 'white noise', whose constituent frequencies are taken from a wide range of the frequency spectrum and presented at the same intensity.

Many studies were successful in finding adverse effects of

noise upon efficiency provided that the noise level employed was at least 90dBA, and that the task involved sustained attention and was prolonged for half an hour or more. The main effect of noise upon performance in such situations was found to be upon accuracy, resulting in an increase in the number of wrong responses made. Furthermore, this loss of accuracy tended to become greater as a function of time at work, while at the beginning of the work period, performance was often better in noise. Usually, subjects were unaware of this increasing loss of efficiency, believing their performance to be as good as ever.

Broadbent and Little (1960) attempted to replicate these laboratory findings in an industrial setting. This study investigated the effects of noise reduction upon the efficiency of operators engaged in film perforation. At the beginning of the investigation, the noise level at the workplace was about 99dBA and this was reduced to 89dBA by placing absorbent material between the machines. Half of the available machines were treated in this way and the remaining half left untreated, so that the efficiency of the same operators, moving from treated to untreated workbays and hence working at the two noise levels, could be compared. Mistakes and equipment shutdowns were greatly reduced in the treated workbays. Apart from the confirmation of some hypotheses generated by laboratory experiments provided by this study, the important finding is that noise effects on efficiency appear in individuals who are accustomed to noise and who have plenty of experience in the work situation. Indeed, in this particular study the effects of noise reduction were considerable and this is possibly due to the presence of an incentives payment scheme.

More recently, it having been established that loud noise can bring about impairments of efficiency, research has been mainly directed at elucidating the mechanism mediating the effects of noise upon efficiency. This has been achieved by making detailed comparisons of the effects of noise and those of other stresses, such as loss of sleep, heat and high levels of incentive, upon the performance of tasks requiring continuous attention, and by observing the changes in efficiency that occur when a man works under two stresses simultaneously.

Loss of sleep, for example, does not produce the same kind of impairment in efficiency that loud noise does. Whereas noise increases the number of wrong responses, sleep deprivation increases the number of lapses of attention. Thus in noise an individual makes *commission errors* – responding incorrectly to presented information – while with loss of sleep he makes *errors of omission* – failing to notice that information requiring action has been presented. However, when an individual deprived of sleep works in noise then the effects of sleep loss are reduced, and he is able to work at normal levels of efficiency, although this probably demands a greater expenditure of effort. Incentives also increase the adverse effects of noise upon efficiency. In other words, noise only impairs the efficiency of men who are highly motivated (for example, if they are working under an incentive payments scheme) and may even improve the performance of individuals who are bored.

Noise and incentives thus seem to resemble one another in some respects and to exert effects in the opposite direction to those of sleeplessness and boredom. These results are usually conceptualized by assuming that there is a general internal state of arousal or reactivity (see A5) which is increased by incentives or by noise and reduced by loss of sleep or by boredom. It is further assumed that inefficiency is high when the arousal level is too high or too low, that is, the relation between efficiency and arousal is thought to follow an inverted U, efficiency being best at an intermediate level.

In some respects, the arousal model is too simple and does not account for some aspects of the experimental results obtained. In particular, the nature of errors at high levels of arousal, as in Broadbent and Little's industrial experiment, is unclear. Recent evidence (Hockey 1970a,b) suggests that loud noise affects some task demands more than others. It produces a structured change in the way in which attention is distributed over the components of a task, resulting in attention becoming more *selective*. Thus the effects of noise will tend to be more apparent in multi-component task situations, where several operations must be carried out, rather than in simple task situations where only one source of information is monitored. Noise thus appears to bias perceptual selection, so

48

that high priority task components receive more attention while low priority task components receive less. Unexpected signals or pieces of information are therefore likely to be inefficiently dealt with. In noise the operator simplifies the task for himself by paying less attention to those sources of information which he regards as unimportant, and probably places undue reliance on habitual, well-learned routines. In consequence, an individual working in noise is likely to be less well-prepared to cope with the unexpected, since he is dealing with the task in hand largely in terms of already formed hypotheses about what will happen. It is possible therefore that accidents may be increased by noise, since they are due in large part to the misperception of potentially dangerous situations (Broadbent, 1970). However, evidence on this point is lacking and the problems involved make research in this area extremely difficult to carry out (Kerr, 1950).

Not surprisingly, noise also tends to impair speech communication and, in noisy surroundings, workers tend to develop coughs, hoarseness, lesions and throat pains from the strain of trying to talk through the noise (Brewer and Briess, 1960). How easily a speaker can be heard depends upon the intensity of his voice compared to the intensity and frequency of the ambient noise. The greatest distance between two speakers at which they can speak to each other with little difficulty is a function of the noise level in dB, averaged over its component frequencies between 600 and 4800 Hz (the speech interference level) and the loudness of their voices. Tables are available which give such information for various speech interference levels, and various voice levels (Morgan, Cook, Chapanis and Lund, 1963). For instance at a speech interference level of 70dB, speakers need to be at a distance of about six inches from each other if they wish to speak normally and be understood. Speech interference levels need to be lower for telephone communication, since the listener cannot see the speaker and the noise source is less easy to avoid. A speech interference level of 60dB produces some difficulty and one of 75dB makes telephonic communication impossible (Poulton, 1970).

Exposure to high intensity noise is frequently thought of as being stressful and individuals exposed to noisy environments

49

might therefore be expected to show abnormalities of endocrine system and cardiovascular system functioning, since both systems come under the control of the autonomic nervous system, which is diffusely involved in reactions to stress (see A2). Exposure to noise does not appear to affect endocrine system functioning significantly; Levi (1967) for example, obtained data suggesting that exposure to industrial noise on the one hand and performing office work on the other both increased the excretion of catecholamines, but a more important influence upon catecholamine excretion was the attitude of the individual to the two situations.

However, some industrial studies have indicated that significantly more workers in noisy than in quiet work environments complain of circulatory, cardiac and equilibrium problems, or suffer from hypertension. Many of these studies seem open to various methodological objections and in any case the contributions of non-noise factors to these differences cannot be ruled out (Kryter, 1970).

Noise has also been thought to exert deleterious effects on workers' mental health. Jansen (1959) examined more than 1000 foundry workers in various parts of Germany. As well as making physiological observations, Jansen also assessed mental health symptoms by means of a clinical interview. The factories from which the workers were drawn were classified in terms of the typical level of noise exposure. Jansen then compared workers exposed to high noise levels with those exposed to lower noise levels and found that the former showed more emotional tension in the home and in the factory. However, this study has been criticized on the grounds that first, the individuals assessed for mental health symptoms were selected in a rather uncontrolled way; second, the methods of assessing symptoms were highly subjective; and third, in any case only a few symptoms, from the large number assessed, distinguished between workers from high and low noise environments.

In a carefully controlled survey of personnel involved in aircraft launch operations aboard US Navy Aircraft Carriers, Davis (1958) found that there appeared to be a consistent tendency for men most exposed to aircraft noise to perform the least well on a variety of psychomotor tasks. These included aspects of steadiness and reaction time. However, over-all there were no completely clear-cut differences between the most exposed and least exposed groups. In addition, psychiatric examination by tests and interview procedures revealed that the most exposed men appeared to experience greater feelings of anxiety. It is possible, however, that the greater anxiety experienced by these men is attributable to the fact that their jobs were more difficult and more dangerous (Kryter, 1970). The presence of intense noise usually implies the presence of powerful machinery which requires highly skilled operation and where mistakes can have dangerous consequences. Thus, the expressed anxiety may relate more to these factors than to the high noise levels. In Davis's study the most exposed personnel did not rate the jet aircraft noise as any more disturbing than did personnel who were less exposed, but they did express more anxiety about the jobs they were doing.

One of the problems inherent in the assessment of the effects of noise on mental health in industrial studies is that of self-selection. Workers who find high noise levels disturbing and in whom symptoms of mental ill-health are perhaps provoked may well leave the job or the industry in question. It is also possible that noisy jobs attract a lower proportion of people who are unstable to begin with and so the effects of noise are masked. Thirdly, although noise may not produce any increase in symptoms, the psychological cost of maintaining apparent stability at work may be very high, and this may reveal itself outside the work situation, for instance at home, or within it in the form of reduced morale. Rodda (1967) has suggested the interesting possibility that personnel in noisy industries, for example the motor manufacturing and shipbuilding industries, may have lower morale, although he admits that there could be many other reasons for this.

Monitoring and inspection work

Since many jobs in automated systems require operators merely to detect whether or not some relatively rare event has occurred, and since quality control procedures in many areas of modern industry require inspectors to work for a number of hours each day trying to spot faults, many laboratory, and some field, studies have been undertaken of the factors thought to be involved in performance in such situations (Davies and Tune, 1970). Most of these studies, or at least those conducted in the laboratory, have clearly indicated that man is a poor monitor. In laboratory studies of monitoring behaviour, the observer typically watches a display for the occurrence of faint and infrequent signals arriving at unpredictable times over a prolonged period. In general the number of signals correctly detected declines, sometimes by as much as 40 per cent, after about half an hour of work, although it has been shown that providing immediate feedback on whether responses are correct or incorrect can either reduce this decline or prevent it altogether. Since in many industrial situations the provision of knowledge of results is not feasible, injecting artificial signals into the task or providing frequent short rest pauses, both of which are known to prevent a decline in performance (Davies, 1970), may be of more practical significance. Hartley, Olsson and Ingleby (see Poulton, 1974) have also indicated the potential usefulness of computer assistance in reducing monitoring decrements. However, attempts to devise selection batteries for efficient monitors have largely failed (McGrath, 1968), although current attempts to devise task taxonomies for monitoring situations may enable some progress in this area to be achieved.

Conclusions

Ergonomics has thus addressed itself to a wide variety of problems affecting human efficiency at work, concentrating principally on those involved in man-machine or man-environment interaction or, more recently, on those involved in viewing man as a system component. However, the view has sometimes been expressed that ergonomics has had a comparatively small impact on industrial practice, at least in Britain, and reasons which have been advanced to explain this state of affairs include the relative lack of awareness of management with respect to ergonomic problems and the shortage of ergonomics specialists in industry (Jackson, 1967).

Finally, it should be noted that up to now ergonomics has

been largely an American and Western European discipline (Chapanis, 1974). As Chapanis points out in considering the importance of national and cultural variables in ergonomics, virtually all ergonomic findings 'apply to large boned peoples, people who were born to or use the English language, and people who have Western customs, habits and ways of life. That is a pretty small percentage of the world's population.' Chapanis provides numerous examples of the difficulties that users, for example in underdeveloped countries, may encounter with equipment designed to meet American and European anatomical and cultural specifications.

Intrinsic motivation and job design

Henry Ford I is quoted as saying in 1922, 'The average worker wants a job in which he does not have to put much physical effort. Above all, he wants a job in which he does not have to think.' Supported by this convenient philosophy, Ford concentrated on minimizing immediate costs by designing jobs to involve as few tasks as possible, to perform a sequence of tasks repeatedly and to reduce all jobs to a minimum skill level so as to reduce learning time for the job. In terms of reduced unit costs, the results of his assembly line procedures were remarkable. In 1909 his first Model T cost $850. By 1926 it sold for only $350 and had a self-starter. Ford paid high wages, too. In 1914 the national average wage in the USA was $2.40 a day. Ford paid a minimum of $5.00.

Critics of the assembly line have pointed to such common features as the social isolation, the high noise level (which is undesirable in itself and further reduces social contact), the limits on promotion opportunities imposed by the minimum skill level required, and the monotony and fatigue associated with paced and repetitive tasks. Most of all they have criticized the loss of a sense of personal achievement in work, caused by the fractionization and specialization of jobs. (It should be noted that the assembly line is not the only example of fractionization and specialization. Many white collar as well as blue collar jobs are designed on these principles, but the assembly line is the most striking example.) Maslow has proposed that most people strive for self-actualization in their jobs and Herzberg has shown the importance of intrinsic aspects of the job, such as gaining responsibility and a sense of achievement, to the worker's satisfaction. Until recently, job design principles have paid comparatively little attention to these needs. The media, too, has been loud in its criticism of the assembly line methods which are seen as dehumanizing the worker (e.g. Charlie Chaplin's film *Modern Times*) and condemning him to a 'prison factory'.

Job rotation

New approaches to job design have been proposed to improve the motivational content of jobs. One alternative is *job rotation* where workers periodically change to a different task on either an obligatory or voluntary basis. The workers are usually assigned to a series of tasks and each worker rotates his job with another at periodic intervals. This method is usually applied when the basic job cannot be modified, and has the advantage of increasing job interest due to changes in the skill requirements and content of the job. But the benefits of job rotation may be outweighed by the disruption of social relationships.

Job enlargement

This is a method whereby two or more separate jobs are combined into one job. An enlarged job is one in which the work is more interesting; the incumbent has more freedom to plan the job and has a reasonable say in how it is done; the job is not too closely supervised, provides feedback and opportunities; and the worker feels it is worthwhile putting effort into the job. The assumption is that the bigger the job, the more intrinsically satisfying it is.

A distinction is sometimes made between *horizontal* and *vertical* job enlargement. Horizontal job enlargement involves extending a person's job outwards at the same level. Instead of adding one piece to an assembly before passing it along, an operative may add several parts or construct the whole assembly. In vertical job enlargement an employee takes over some of the responsibility previously held by a superior. For example, where a worker once produced a part and then passed it on for inspection by someone else, he may do the producing and the inspecting. It could be, though, that in such a situation, one person's job enlargement is another person's job impoverishment. Job enrichment is a term often used synonymously with vertical job enlargement but is perhaps rather unfortunate since it implies the addition of special factors or ingredients to a job which affect satisfaction and productivity. Rather, it is the overall structure of the working environment which affects the quality of working life. Job enlargement, job enrichment and job rotation can best be viewed as different ways of designing or redesigning (restructuring) work to consider the needs of the individual and increase its intrinsically-motivating properties.

The results of such job restructuring are said to include increased worker satisfaction, reduced absenteeism, reduced labour turnover and increased output. In fact, some of the well-known job restructuring programmes on assembly lines were prompted not so much by humanitarian reasons or by a desire on the part of management for increased output, but from problems of high absenteeism, high labour turnover and difficulties of recruiting workers for assembly line jobs. Empirical studies of the effects of job restructuring have shown mixed results. Although a considerable number of studies have been reported, few show evidence of thorough experimental investigation. Few studies have used control groups and often only slight attention has been paid to an evaluation of benefits.

One of the better studies in this respect was conducted at ICI Limited by Paul, Robertson and Herzberg (1969). One group of subjects of the investigation were laboratory technicians who were suffering from low morale. Two groups of employees were studied – an experimental group whose jobs were 'enriched' and a matched control group. Neither group was told that they were to be the subject of study to avoid the 'Hawthorne effect' (the tendency for people to behave differently when they know that they are being studied). 'Hygiene' factors were held constant, meaning that matters such as pay, working conditions and security remained unchanged, but 'motivator' factors were improved. Thus, the technicians were encouraged to write final reports on any research project for which they had been responsible and permitted authority to order supplies which gave an opportunity for increased responsibility and recognition of achievement. They were given opportunities for self-initiated work which gave scope for personal growth and they became involved in planning projects and setting targets. All these changes were designed to give chances for achievement and to make the work more challenging.

All the subjects were asked to write monthly reports of the work done, which were used as a measure of work performance. The quality of the reports of the experimental group soon outpaced that of the control group and almost all the experimental group reports were judged as good as those of the research scientists. However, measures of job satisfaction were no higher at the end of the trial period than they were at the beginning, although Paul et al (1969) conclude, 'There is every reason to think that in the long term attitudes will catch up with performance'.

Other investigators have found that satisfaction has increased, with performance remaining unchanged, while another consistent finding is that output stays unchanged or is even reduced but quality improves. It is probable, therefore, that many factors related to the job, the organization and the employees, affect the success of job restructuring. For example, there is evidence that the view that everyone would welcome additional responsibility and bigger jobs is an oversimplification. If an enlarged job brings the worker additional fatigue or tension and a reduced opportunity to daydream he may be less satisfied than he was with a routine job. Blood and Hulin (1967) showed a negative correlation between satisfaction and job complexity for blue collar workers in urban locations and a positive relationship for workers from rural locations. This implies that workers from a rural location would respond more positively to an enlarged job than would urban workers. The authors attribute the differences to the alienation of city workers from the work norms of the middle classes. City workers reject the idea that work has intrinsic merit.

Consistent with these findings are the results of a study by Hackman and Lawler (1971). They demonstrated that a positive relationship between enlarged jobs and favourable outcomes (in terms of satisfaction, low absenteeism and high quality work) is primarily a characteristic of those who value higher-order need satisfaction. It is likely that it is these individuals who will respond most favourably to job enlargement. It seems that the relationship between jobs, workers and organizations is a complex one which defies easy answers. It is a question which will be examined in more detail in Chapter 6.

Pay and behaviour

Pay is a much more common method of attempting to motivate good performance at work than is job enlargement. Campbell *et al* (1970) surveyed thirty-three industrial companies in the USA and reported that every organization attempted to use money as a motivator of effective management performance while almost none of their respondents followed a conscious policy of designing jobs so that they would be stimulating, challenging or a rewarding experience. One personnel manager voiced the view that 'We're not in business to make people happy'. This section examines how pay is associated with the behaviour and satisfaction of individuals. The section does not look at different payment systems which might be selected, but rather examines some of the factors associated with the use of pay and some empirical work on its effects.

Incentive payment systems
Incentive plans are based on behavioural criteria such as the output of an individual or group, rather than on factors of age, experience or skills. Measures of output usually rest in turn on a time-study programme, which attempts to arrive at a standard time for any given task. With non-salaried personnel, field studies of incentive plans have shown that they do tend to increase performance (i.e. greater output per man hour) when they are instituted. The plans also result in lower unit costs and higher wages in comparison with straight payment systems. However, installing such schemes frequently results in attendant changes in management policies and work methods so that it is difficult to know how much of the im-

provement is due to changes in payment methods. Controlled laboratory experiments of the effects of different methods of payment on workers may help to resolve this problem, but there are few studies of this nature.

However, it is probable that incentive plans are never as effective as they might be in increasing performance since they are often of such a nature that workers are totally unaware of how the incentive system works, and so rarely understand how their incentive pay is determined. If workers are unaware of how the system works, and how the pay they receive every week is determined, it is not surprising that incentive systems fail to work effectively.

A second reason that incentive plans fail to increase performance is the 'rate restriction' phenomenon (see Ch. 6). Thus, the influence of group production norms may mean that a worker prefers to restrict his output rather than tolerate the disapproval or ostracism which often accompanies being a 'rate buster'.

Managerial pay curves

While there are many speculations about the effect of salary policy on employee behaviour, and while most managers see pay as a principal factor in motivating individuals, there is little empirical evidence to go on. The existing studies have usually relied on longitudinal data of managers' salary changes over a period of years. Plotting these salary figures yields a pay curve for each individual, and one can examine how organizations have been using pay over the years. Haire, Ghiselli and Gordon (1967) examined the salary history of managers from three firms over a twenty-five-year period. Pay positively accelerated with time, that is, pay increases became larger and larger, on the average, as the years went by. But the variability of pay also increased with time. One could infer from these findings that an organization believes that a manager's contribution to the company becomes greater year by year, and rewards appropriately. But there was evidence that many managers changed their position in the 'salary scale' relative to other managers, since present pay was not a good predictor of future pay. If the relative position of the managers had remained constant, pay would have been a good predictor of subsequent pay. In fact, in two of the three companies the pay increases seem to have been distributed, judging from the statistical evidence alone, in a random manner.

There are two interpretations of this study. If one assumes that performance is consistent within individuals, then the random distribution of pay increases can be taken as evidence that the companies do not consistently reward good performance. On the other hand, the change in relative rank of the managers might show that the company *does* reward good performance but that individuals' motivations and abilities change over time.

Salary secrecy

A study by Lawler (1967) indicates that the secrecy which often surrounds the amount of pay an individual receives may affect satisfaction and possibly performance. He found that, in conditions of salary secrecy, managers overestimated the pay of subordinates and peers, and underestimated their superiors' pay. Thus, there is a general tendency to underestimate the size of differentials, whether one looks up the job structure or down it. Senior managers are less satisfied with the differentials since they overestimate what their juniors are earning. While junior people may feel happier about the differentials because they underestimate what their superiors are earning, it may also reduce their incentive to seek promotion. Another disadvantage of secrecy is that it lowers money's effectiveness as a method of providing knowledge-of-results to let managers know how well they are doing. It would seem to be advantageous, in many respects, to abandon secret pay policies. However, this might well be inadvisable if a company's remuneration policies are riddled with anomalies and inequities as a result of inadequate job-performance appraisal systems, and fail to reflect a valid relationship between pay and performance.

Sociotechnical systems

Any industrial production system involves both a basic technology – the plant, raw materials, machinery and processes involved in production – and a social organization which relates the workers in the system to each other and to their tasks. The *sociotechnical* approach to the study of work differs from those reviewed earlier in this chapter in that it is concerned specifically with the *interaction* between technical and social aspects of work organization. As Cooper and Foster (1970) have expressed it: 'The technology makes demands and places limits on the type of work structure possible, while the work structure itself has social and psychological properties which generate their own unique requirements with regard to the task to be done.' The interactions concern both the individual worker and the work group in relation to task demands; we shall consider both here, although Cooper and Foster have suggested that individual task interaction should be termed 'psycho-technical' and the label 'socio-technical' reserved for interaction analysis at the group level.

It seems clear (e.g. Woodward, 1958) that distinct types of technology produce rather different types of social system. In *mass production*, for example, the operator's relation to his task is generally mechanical. His job is repetitive and 'short-cycle', more often than not paced and controlled by the machine and by the speed of the conveyor belt rather than by himself. Tasks are subdivided in allocation. The social implication is that operators work in isolation, spatially and temporally separated from one another. They lose sight of the end product of the system, and working groups, either in terms of common motivation or in terms of spatial or temporal closeness, are hard to form. Supervision, on the other hand, is normally close, and discipline and pressure towards the production quota are considerable.

By contrast, in *process production* the work process is more or less automated – for example, in production of chemicals or of petroleum. Here the operator is more in control of his machine; the machine performs its own work and the operator's role is basically that of monitor and, perhaps, manual operator in case of failure. The relation between man and machine is, therefore, complementary and the operator to some extent autonomous. Supervisory pressure tends to be less, and individual responsibility greater, than in mass production.

The growth of automation, which tends to be a change

from mass production to process production, produces changes in the social system at work which are both good and bad. The foregoing descriptions have made some 'good' consequences evident: with automation the operator is in control of, rather than controlled by, his machine; he is less under supervision, more under specialist guidance; he may feel autonomy and increased individual responsibility to be both intrinsically satisfying and status-enhancing. On the other hand, although he is more free to leave his machine than the mass-production worker is to leave the conveyor belt, he may still work very much in isolation from other operators; he is still likely to have little or no sight of the end product of the system; and, while the physical demands of work may be less than in mass production, the perceptual demands of monitoring and increased personal responsibility for breakdown may impose considerable psychological strain. Further social strains are imposed by shift systems, which are most prevalent in process industries where plant must be kept running continuously. The shift system means that family and other social relations outside work are disrupted by abnormal or erratic working hours, and tend to be replaced by social relations within the work shift; but the stress and isolation of the work situation may make even such social relations difficult to form.

We have already said that technical and social systems are said to *interact*. If work characteristics influence the type of social structure which can exist within a given industrial system, it is also true that the type of social structure itself has repercussions upon the work situation – in particular, upon productivity and upon the likelihood of work disturbances (strikes being the most dramatic example). A classification of types of work group has been suggested by Sayles (1958), who distinguishes four basic types termed 'erratic', 'apathetic', 'strategic' and 'conservative'. Group type, he argues, is determined by technology: in particular by such factors as the status of the group in the hierarchy of the 'parent' industry; its size and the variability of functions and members within it; the degree of repetitiveness of its work and the degree of individual responsibility assumed; and the degree to which its work is essential to the overall production system. 'Strategic' work groups, for example, which are generally formed among operators employed in essential sections of the production system, are more often militant, and more likely to strike, than other groups – perhaps not surprisingly, since their power, in terms of threatened shutdown, is generally greater. As other writers, too, have pointed out (e.g. Cooper and Foster, 1970), when technological change entails a loss of individual or small-group control, a lessened sight of the end product, and a reduced versatility of functions of group members, one result is often a low productivity norm. Cooper and Foster suggest that this functions as a defence against work disturbances – both technical and social – beyond the operators' control. We have also seen, in Chapter 2, that individual job satisfaction, while it may not be closely correlated with individual performance, tends to reduce absenteeism, job leaving (with its result of costly replacement training) and perhaps accident rate. Concern for the social consequences of technical systems is therefore a result not only of altruism but also of practical economics.

What are the implications of the socio-technical approach for work design? Generalizations, particularly with respect to individual motivation, must be made with the greatest caution. Nevertheless, it seems possible to argue that for high productivity and high job satisfaction a desirable technical system is one which will in turn create a social system of the following type. Working groups feel some collective responsibility and autonomy for a job section which is in some sense a meaningful whole; there is both interdependence and variability of tasks carried out within a group; and the individual operator can, to some extent, experience a challenge, can feel that his own qualities of judgement and decision are relevant and valued and can feel that he is in control of his task and not controlled by it.

Such a technical system may not easily be achieved. Woodward's (1958) first category of industrial technology – the one-off or *unit* production system, as distinct from mass production and process production – might be said to come close to it. In this system (typified by locomotive manufacture) groups or teams of skilled craftsmen work closely together, often for a considerable period of time, on a single product whose completion is clearly seen by all team members and for which responsibility is collective. In other types of production it may be possible to bring technical and social organization as far as possible into harmony, and to devise working groups which are given, as Cooper and Foster term it, 'responsible autonomy'. Some Scandinavian car manufacturing companies appear to be moving in this direction, and have completely redesigned the car assembly line. As a result (*pace* the Hawthorne effect!) absenteeism and turnover rates appear to have dramatically declined.

4
Selection and guidance

Selection of an individual for a job is really a problem of prediction; it involves predicting which of the individuals that apply for a particular job are best able to perform that job. It is in the interests of both the organization seeking to engage an individual, and in the interests of the individual himself, that this prediction is as reliable and valid as possible. If methods are available which allow the selection of those potential job-holders who are likely to be the most productive, then the average productivity of the organization is likely to rise; the applicant benefits by being placed in a job which suits his interests and needs; and both the organization and the individual benefit by having a job-holder who is interested in and satisfied with his job.

But selection is only one element in the whole process of an organization's effective utilization of manpower. Fig. 4.1 gives a simplified overview of the main phases of the process.

It can be seen that the process often begins with an analysis of the job itself, in terms of a job description. This job description should specify the conditions of work, the operations performed, equipment used, amount and nature of training required, rate of pay, relation to other jobs and other pertinent information. A personnel requisition can be specified from this analysis and usually includes such job requirements as the

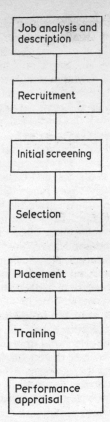

Fig. 4.1 *Steps in the selection and placement process*

type of experience, age, educational level and skills needed by the job-holder.

The recruiting stage can then proceed. Advertisements for the job vacancy might be placed in local or national papers, on the television, in professional magazines, or a 'trawl' could be made within the organization itself. Decisions on which media to use will depend on the acceptable cost of recruitment to the organization and the number and type of potential job applicants (the 'selection ratio'). Unskilled and semiskilled workers, for example, usually tend to work near their place of residence and an advertisement in a local paper is often sufficient if there is no local shortage of such labour. Oil companies wishing to recruit oil pipe-laying specialists with experience of pipe-laying in rough sea conditions, on the other hand, may have to advertise on an international scale and accept such costs as international travel expenses while attending interviews and the successful applicant's removal expenses.

In the first example, the selection ratio is low, or favourable (that is, there is a large number of potential applicants relative to the number of vacancies) and the recruitment costs are small. In the case of the vacancy for an oil pipe-laying specialist, the selection ratio is unfavourable and the costs high.

When sufficient applicants have been found for a vacancy, an initial screening usually takes place. This may include a study by a panel of the applicants' biographical details such as age, experience, education, etc., and the contacting of referees for their comments on the applicant. Prospective jobholders are then 'short-listed' or ranked and a number of them move on to the next step in the process – the selection stage.

Techniques that are available to aid the personnel psychologist in predicting the future success of an applicant include selection tests, the selection interview, application forms and reference checks. Each of these methods will be examined in this chapter, but first it is important to consider two major requirements of a 'good' test or measure – its reliability and validity – so as to have some basis for an evaluation of the worth of each of these four techniques (see D4).

Reliability

A good test or measure must be reliable. That is, the test must be consistent in the answers that it gives. Reliability is defined as the degree to which two separate, independent measurements of the same thing agree with one another and this measure of agreement is usually expressed by a co-efficient of correlation which represents the relationship between the two sets of measurements. Three measures of reliability are usually recognized, test-retest reliability, internal consistency and equivalent forms. The test-retest reliability (or 'stability') of a test is the extent to which two administrations of the same test to the same applicants yield the same results. If exactly the same score were achieved by each applicant at both testings, then the test would be perfectly reliable (i.e. the co-efficient of stability would be 1.00). To illustrate the concepts of test-retest reliability, Morgan (1961) gives the example of a professor marking examination papers. One way the professor could assign a grade to each of the papers would be to throw the whole set downstairs, and assign a grade to each paper based on the step on which it landed. If the professor then wanted to test the reliability of his method of marking, he would pick up the papers and throw them down the stairs again in exactly the same way as he had done the first time. The chances are that the grade for each paper on this second 'testing' would bear very little relation to the score obtained on the first grading. The method would therefore be considered unreliable.

A second way to consider the reliability of a test is to measure its internal consistency. This involves dividing the test into two parts and correlating the scores on one part with those on the other. There are a number of ways in which a test can be divided. A common way is to correlate the first half of the test with the second half to yield a *split-half correlation*. Or the odd numbered test items can be correlated with the even numbered ones to yield an *odd-even correlation*. A high correlation on these methods (i.e. high internal consistency) means that each item of the test represents a slightly different way of measuring the same thing.

A third type of reliability is equivalent forms reliability which involves the construction of two forms of the same test. The correlation between scores on the two tests is known as the co-efficient of equivalence. It is usually relatively easy to construct a different form of a test, since theoretically a test only contains a selection of all possible items which could be included, and the availability of another version of the same test often has many practical advantages. For example, applicants often cannot be given the same test twice, since practice effects may interfere, but there may not be this problem with a second version of the same test. The use of an equivalent form also has the advantage of compensating for possible errors made by the test constructor in sampling from all possible items.

Validity

A good test or measure must also be valid. In the simplest case, validation is 'testing the test' and refers to how well a test measures what it is intended or purports to measure. A test may be a highly reliable measure of something which is internally consistent but the test may fail to correlate with the intended external criteria. The correlation of test scores with external criteria yields measures of test validity. As with test reliability, more than one form of test validity is usually recognized – content, empirical and construct validity. Although a different process is used to establish the validity in each of these three cases, each relies on some *criterion* with which the test correlates.

Content validity. This refers to the extent to which the test is a good sample of the behaviours, skills or knowledge which the test purports to measure. In this case the criterion is essentially a subjective matter, since it usually involves asking experts to judge whether the test or item did assess a particular attribute of the examinee. Face validity is often considered as a variation of content validity. A test is said to have face validity, if it *appears* to measure particular attributes of individuals. So-called personality tests in magazines rely heavily on face validity, though there is no guarantee that a test which seems 'on the face of it' to measure some aspect of behaviour does in fact do so. In some situations, however, it may be important that a test has face validity in addition to the usual requirements of high reliability and test validity. Performance at a pursuit rotor task may be a valid measure of skill as a car driving instructor, but a test with so little face validity may cause resentment, criticism and lack of motivation on the part of job applicants.

Empirical validity. Establishing the empirical validity (sometimes referred to as criterion-related validity) is usually a prime concern of test constructors, and refers to the extent to which a test correlates with either a current or future attribute of a testee. *Concurrent validity* is the extent to which a test correlates with a currently available criterion measure; the *predictive* validity of a test is the degree to which it correlates with some criterion measure obtained some time after the test has been administered. Thus the empirical validity of a test battery intended to predict the success of export salesmen might be judged against the scores of currently employed export salesmen with good sales records. This would give us the concurrent validity of the test battery. Alternatively, we might wait until the examinees had been in their new job as export salesmen for some years, and correlate their scores on the tests at entry with their sales figures two years later, which would establish the predictive validity of the test.

An obvious difficulty in establishing the predictive validity of a test is that it takes many years to collect on-the-job performance data for even one employee, and a relatively large number of people is required for validity studies to be conducted. One type of empirical validity called simulated validity can often be employed to avoid some of these problems. As the name implies, obtaining simulated validity data on a test, or test battery, involves designing a simulation of the job in which the appropriate criterion data can be collected. Obviously some jobs are easier to simulate than others, but a set of tasks, involving perhaps a couple of days at each task, could be constructed. Performance at each of these tasks can be carefully measured. Using the measures as criterion data allows us to establish the simulated predictive validity of the initial tests.

Construct validity. The construct validity of a measure is how well it connects with a theoretical construct which in turn is linked to other observable measurements and constructs. Thus construct validity is calculated when the attribute to be measured is a general dimension of differences between individuals such as extraversion, neuroticism, intelligence or anxiety. Such a dimension is usually an intervening variable or hypothetical construct within an explanatory theory and derives its definition from its place in the theory.

One method of establishing construct validity is through

correlational or factor analytic techniques. A particular theory should state predictions about the relationships between constructs. If tests purporting to measure constructs correlate in the predicted direction then the validity of the test as a measure of a construct within the theory is supported.

Selection tests

Tests have been proposed to measure individual differences for thousands of years. Plato proposed a series of tests for the selection of the guardians of his ideal republic and the mandarin bureaucracy of China was selected on the basis of scholarship and test achievement. But it was not until the First World War and the need to screen large numbers of men for the Forces that interest in the development of group tests was stimulated. For example, the Army Alpha and Army Beta (for non-literates) intelligence tests were used in the USA to screen hundreds of thousands of men and to place them in jobs ranging from labour battalions to special services. By the breakout of the Second World War many of the tests that are in use today had been developed.

Tests of aptitude, ability, interests and personality are often used to provide information about job applicants which can be used as a basis for selection decisions. Among the most common standardized *aptitude tests* are tests of vision, hearing, simple motor skills, clerical aptitude, and mechanical comprehension. *Achievement or ability tests* measure current proficiency and include written information tests, tests of job skills such as typing and dictation, and handling matters in a manager's or administrator's in-basket.

The use of any selection technique requires that the personality traits, abilities or other characteristics which are responsible for success or failure in a job can be identified. So before reaching for an 'off-the-shelf' test, or constructing one for use in selection, it is important to decide what are the important attributes for job success and whether criteria are available to check the validity of the measures. In a review of the validity of occupational aptitude tests, for example, Ghiselli (1966) showed that intelligence tests predicted success in training in many types of skilled work such as electric workers, computing clerks and process workers, while non-intellectual tests of dexterity had little or no validity in predicting success in training. On the other hand, dexterity tests predicted trainability in observational and manipulative occupations like inspectors, packers and bench assembly workers, while intelligence tests had little or no validity.

A job applicant's personality and interests are also likely to affect his success in many jobs. Obviously, an applicant with gregarious tendencies is unlikely to be satisfied in a job with very little opportunity for personal contact. But unlike aptitude and ability tests, *personality and interest tests* have found their greatest application in non-manual jobs. The more a job requires working with others, the more it is complex and the more discretion allowed the job incumbent, the more personality and interest assessments are likely to add to the ability to predict occupational success.

Unfortunately, there is some doubt about whether valid data of an applicant's personality can be obtained using standardized paper-and-pencil tests in an industrial selection setting, when the applicant obviously wants to appear as good a candidate as possible. Heron (1956) administered a questionnaire to 200 applicants for the post of bus conductor as part of the selection procedure and the same questionnaire to a second group of 200 immediately *after* the selection procedure, when the applicants were told that they were helping with a research project. This second group appeared significantly more emotionally maladjusted, from the questionnaire scores, than those who had taken the test for selection purposes. It seems from this that the selection group was not willing to admit socially undesirable traits in the selection situation. Projective tests (in which a person is asked to give meaning to or tell a story about a relatively ambiguous stimulus such as a picture) also are able to be faked in a similar way.

Forced choice personality tests, which ask the respondent to choose between two equally desirable or equally undesirable traits the one which is more true of himself, represent one attempt that has been made to avoid the fakability problem. The disadvantage of this method is that a respondent may resent or resist having to choose from two socially undesir-

71

able statements the one which is closer to himself, and may refuse to answer.

Situational tests, such as in-basket tests and the Leaderless Group Discussion, are other methods of minimizing faking. In-basket tests are used to select applicants for executive or administrative positions and present the candidate with a hypothetical problem represented by memos, reports and letters in his 'in-basket'. The candidate must tackle the problem by dictating memos and letters, arranging meetings, etc., just as he would on the job. In the leaderless group discussion (LGD), a group of candidates are assigned a topic for discussion, usually on a job-related topic so as to increase face validity, with a specified period of time in which to discuss it. Examinees act as observers and some objective scoring techniques have been constructed, giving good inter-judge and test-retest reliability. Although both in-basket tests and the LGD have not been shown to be valid for assessing broad personality traits, they have proved valid in predicting performance in supervisory and administrative jobs.

One selection test, of whatever type, is rarely an adequate predictor of job success, and a common practice is to use a variety of tests. Since the validity coefficient of a single test is usually lower than .40 it can be appreciated that one test measures only a small part of the prerequisite for a particular job. Moreover, selection tests are not the only means employed to select applicants. They are one method among a range of techniques each of which, hopefully, adds more reliable and valid information upon which a decision can be based. The selection interview is another of these techniques.

The selection interview

The interview is the most popular selection technique in current use despite the fact that more than fifty years of research has shown that the unstandardized interview has little or no reliability or validity. Henderson (1947) showed that when the objectives of the interview were poorly defined and no systematic schedule of questions was employed, the reliability of assessments was likely to be low, and a review of 80 studies by Mayfield (1964) concluded that there was little evidence for the utility of the interview for predicting an applicant's success in a job and that only intelligence could be predicted satisfactorily from an unstandardized interview.

The continuing popularity enjoyed by the face-to-face interview as a method of screening must be accounted for, therefore, by reasons other than that of its reliability and validity. Ignorance of the research findings on the part of those responsible for selection may be one of the reasons. From the applicant's point of view, he may expect and desire to be interviewed, and an interview has the advantage of allowing him to learn what will be expected of him on the job, to have his queries answered and to meet his potential colleagues. There are advantages, too, as far as the interviewer is concerned. The interview is a behaviour sample and as such allows the interviewer to observe directly certain traits such as voice, speech, nervous mannerisms and general appearance which an organization may feel are important requirements in a job. For example, recruiters often consider personal appearance as an important dimension despite lack of evidence that this relates to success. Conducting an interview also allows the interviewer to feel in control of the process of selection to a greater extent than relying solely on application forms or selection tests. But the interview probably acts more as a mechanism to reject obviously unsuitable applicants rather than as an aid in predicting the future success of the remaining applicants.

Nevertheless, there are conditions under which the accuracy with which interviews can predict later performance can be improved. Interviews which are standardized, presenting the same series of questions to each applicant, have been shown to have a respectable degree of between-judge consistency. Schwab and Heneman (1969) showed that there was a high degree of inter-rater reliability among 18 experienced interviewers who each interviewed the same 5 job applicants in a structured interview situation. (This does, of course, not necessarily mean that they are more accurate.) There was no significant agreement among the same interviewers using an unstructured interview. The validity of an interview can be improved if it is focused, so that the interviewer focuses his questions on a few predetermined attributes. Thus the interview has been shown to be valid for predicting the traits of intelligence, sociability, social adjustment, motivation and interpersonal competence, but only when it was focused. Giving the interview specific behavioural objectives in this way can make it a useful part of the selection process, since it will then provide a unique contribution to supplement the other methods. Even so, many of the traits that can be gauged by the interviewer in a focused interview may be more validly measured by available standardized tests.

Apart from the form of the interview, the interviewer himself is a second major factor determining the reliability and validity of the interview. In many companies personnel interviews are conducted by people with little or no training in interviewing techniques. The effect of training can be to reduce interviewers' biases and idiosyncrasies by alerting the trainees to their existence. One such bias is the 'contagious bias', which refers to the effect that an interviewer's beliefs, expectations or preconceived notions may have on the interview. The term was first used by Rice (1929) who reported a study of 2,000 homeless men and the reasons they gave for their destitution. Although the men were randomly assigned to interviewers, the reasons given depended remarkably on the interviewer. Among those interviewed by an ardent prohibitionist, 34 per cent of the men cited liquor as a cause of their difficulties while 43 per cent cited industrial conditions. In contrast, among those interviewed by an investigator with a 'socialist' bias 11 per cent cited liquor and 60 per cent gave industrial conditions as the cause of their present condition.

Biases may form very early in an interview and the interviewer may be prepared to make his decision after only two or three minutes of interaction. It appears that the usual sequence of events is for the interviewer to form an impression of the applicant and to look for confirmation of this impression. The interviewer has by then committed himself to accept or reject the candidate and the remaining interview is either a formality or merely permits the interviewer to select further consonant information about the applicant.

Application forms are another common method of personnel selection. The information obtained from these forms, such as the applicant's biographical details, his employment history, his education and training and so on, has long been the subject of investigation in order to determine the relationship of these variables to subsequent job performance. Bridgman (1930) for example, examined the relationship between educational achievement and salary earned in a large US company. College grades made relatively little difference to salary on entry, but they were substantially related to advancement in the company and to ultimate job level. Baier and Dugan (1957) showed that the amount of insurance owned by life insurance salesmen was related to success in selling insurance and similarly reported that the amount of insurance owned at time of application for the agent's job was predictive of later performance criteria.

Studies such as these emphasize that items for application blanks should be selected only through an empirical validation of specific responses against a criterion of job success. The items can form the basis of scoring keys to be used with future applicants, and the scoring keys can be cross-validated with new samples of applicants. Unfortunately application form items are all too often selected merely on the basis of their face validity and with no attempt at empirical validation.

When properly constructed the application form has a number of advantages over other forms of selection. It is cheap and easy to administer. It has face validity in the sense that it asks questions which are obviously related to the job. Its use may therefore not be open to criticisms of prying into irrelevant personal matters as the user of personality tests may be accused of doing. Application forms are generally not falsified, in contrast to personality and interest inventories. Finally, many studies have shown the value of application forms in predicting those individuals who will become short-tenure or long-tenure employees, and in predicting job success in such diverse fields of work as maintenance mechanics, salesmen, clerical employees, research scientists and high-level executives.

Reference checks

A fourth common technique used in selection is the reference check, either by letter or telephone, to obtain information about the candidate from persons acquainted with him. Present and previous employers of the candidate are most usually contacted, but there is little reported research to show how valid or reliable these reports might be. A present employer may deliberately falsify his opinion of a candidate in order to be rid of an incompetent worker or a trouble-maker. On the other hand, his reputation as a recommender may suffer if he does so. As a result, recommenders often merely point out favourable points and omit those that are unfavourable to the candidate, which is a process that should incline one to the view that the validity of this method of selection is unlikely to be high!

Like the interview and application form, it is probable that *standardized* recommendation questionnaires have advantages over the letter written in response to an enquiry from an employer. Such questionnaires often include questions on punctuality, attendance, reasons for leaving, etc., and can form the basis of valid keys for forecasting success in specific jobs. The few studies that have been conducted with such standardized recommendation questionnaires have shown only modest validity coefficients, but a full evaluation of the method must await further research.

Vocational guidance

So far in this chapter we have considered selection mostly from an organization's point of view, as if the applicant being interviewed or tested had merely passively arrived at the industrial psychologist's door by chance. But of course, not only do organizations select individuals for jobs, but people select occupations and the type of organization they work for by 'self-selecting' themselves to be screened and by making a second decision once they understand what the job entails. Questions such as the determinates of career choice, the personality patterns characteristic of persons in different occupations and the relationship of occupations to job satisfaction are among those that have been longstanding topics of research in psychology. The topic of career choice has an obvious importance because of the central role played by work in the lives of most individuals. In fact, in selecting an occupation the individual chooses a way of life. The occupation of an individual is an important determinant of his social status. When presented with lists of occupational titles, most people can readily rank the occupations in terms of status, and there is a large degree of agreement between individuals in their rankings. Hierarchical ordering of occupations may be based on the degree of intelligence required, the relative importance to the survival of society, the degree of power over others, length of training or education required, working conditions, and monetary compensation.

Not only ascribed status is determined by occupation. The income from a person's employment to a large extent determines his standard and style of living such as the house he occupies, his recreational activities, his eating and drinking habits, the type of education he chooses for his children, and so on. An occupation can determine the clothing one wears such as the casual attire of a student, the businessman's suit or the chauffeur's uniform. A person's friends, acquaintances and even marriage partner are often met through work. In short, the influence of an occupation extends far beyond the time actually spent at work and into one's whole life.

Guidance of an individual in his choice of occupation has long been a topic of concern to psychologists. The publication in 1909 of *Choosing a Vocation* (Parsons, 1909) can be said to be the starting point of modern vocational guidance, but it was the Great Depression which stimulated much activity, particularly in the USA, with the development of occupational classifications such as the *Dictionary of Occupational Titles* (1939) and with the development of techniques for counselling the unemployed for new occupations. But many of the strides that have been made since that time have been theoretical advances rather than practical ones, though this is not to say that these advances are unimportant, since an occupational psychologist is less able to guide an individual in his career choice if the influences on these choices are unknown.

Lancashire (1971) distinguishes two types of theorists in

the field of occupational choice – the 'differentialists' and the 'developmentalists'. The differentialists have been concerned to study to what extent and in what ways people in one field of work differ from those in another while the developmentalists have explored how any one individual develops ideas about work in general and the stages associated with the development and modification of these ideas.

The differentialist theorists have taken as a starting point the assumption that individuals differ in intelligence, interests, personality, values, motives and so on and that different jobs have different requirements in terms of these constructs. Occupational choice therefore becomes a matching process. For example, Roe (1957) has proposed that personality, emotional needs and value systems are a major determinant of occupational choice, and that these factors are rooted in childhood. According to Roe, protecting or demanding parental attitudes predispose an individual to choose occupations dealing with people, while neglecting, rejecting or casual parental attitudes predispose him to seek occupations dealing with things. However, empirical tests of this hypothesis have generally failed to support it (e.g. Grigg, 1959).

One reason for this may be the serious methodological weakness of these investigations in relying on subjects' recollections of childhood conditions. A longitudinal approach would provide a better test of the hypotheses. Roe's work is also open to criticism in its assumption that occupational choice can be accounted for by the use of one bi-polar factor. Characterizing the family environment in terms of one factor such as warmth, or in terms of the categories of protection or rejection, may be an oversimplification.

Many other investigators have studied personality differences among occupational groups but again much of this type of work is open to methodological criticism. Few studies have used control groups, for example (see A8), so it is often impossible to determine whether personality traits associated with one occupation are characteristic of that occupation or whether they are typical of men that are members of a particular class, or at a certain age, or with a particular level of education, and so on. Where control groups are employed, it is often impossible to establish cause-effect relations to determine the extent to which men with particular personality patterns select certain jobs, and the extent to which personality traits are emphasised by the demands of jobs.

Among the better known work, notable as a longitudinal study which therefore avoids some of these pitfalls, are Terman's studies of children with initial IQs on the Stanford-Binet test of 140 or higher. Terman (1954) showed that men who eventually became physical scientists differed in childhood from those who adopted occupations in the social sciences, the humanities and law on many interest items, including in- dications of childhood interest in scientific matters. Similarly, Levine and Wallen (1954) showed that high school boys who expressed a high degree of interest in one of the interest areas assessed by the Kuder Preference Record were likely to have an occupation in that area seven to nine years later.

Lancashire (1971) identifies a second group of theorists as the 'developmentalists' who have emphasised vocational *development* by pointing out that vocational decisions are made over a period of years, not merely at any one point in time. The best known advocate of this view is Super (1957) who has attempted to divide working life in terms of stages. Super describes five stages in the process of vocational adjust- ment – the growth, exploration, establishment, maintenance and decline stages. The growth stage extends from birth to about fourteen years of age during which time the child begins to develop a 'self concept' through observation of and identi- fication with others (see C3). Needs and fantasies dominate this period but the child takes the first step in vocational development by recognizing that an occupational role can meet his needs.

The exploratory stage covers adolescence and early adult- hood. This period is one of reality testing, with the sub- sequent modification of the self concept and its translation into occupational terms. Because tentative vocational choices are made at this stage, vocational counselling has usually con- centrated on this stage of the development process.

After part-time or trial jobs comes the establishment stage, when a person typically settles at one occupation and assimi- lates the way of life associated with that occupation. The fourth stage is one of 'maintenance' when the individual attempts to retain his established position in the society, while the final stage is an occupational 'decline' with a reduction of occupationally-related activity and eventual retirement.

Super's work has been criticized for not clearly defining the 'self-concept', so central to his work, for not tying the findings of his studies of career patterns to his theoretical approach, and for the over-general nature of this approach (Carkhuff, 1967). Any attempt to describe stages of human development is also open to the suggestion that it is an oversimplification. A development process is continuous, and any description of it in terms of stages is an approximation. Also, there are wide differences in the length of time an individual remains at a particular stage. Some individuals may miss out one or more stages altogether, such as those individuals who remain professionally active long after other people have retired. Gladstone and Winston Churchill are obvious examples. But these limitations are recognized by Super (1957) himself. The importance of his work lies in pointing up developmental sequences, in describing tendencies typical of different periods in life and in providing a stimulus for the formulation and testing of hypotheses for research.

Both the differentialist and the developmentalist approaches have important practical applications in the field of occupational guidance. The developmentalist's stress on occupational choice as a gradual process, continuing right through the working life, has encouraged a move away from vocational guidance at one point in a person's career (usually at school-leaving age) and towards life-span counselling. All-age vocational guidance can be particularly useful following entry into work for an individual who finds that he has made an unsuitable choice, or whose needs have changed, or who has suffered a physical or psychological disablement. In rapidly changing societies many jobs cease to be needed to their former extent, or even disappear altogether, and vocational guidance and retraining of the incumbent, becomes increasingly important.

Work that has stressed the importance of personality, needs, values and the self-concept on occupational choice has brought vocational guidance away from the naive matching of an individual's intelligence and interests to a job chosen by the adviser. Rather, a host of variables such as the client's view of himself, the stage he has reached in the development of thinking about his possible career, his values and in particular the importance he attaches to work in his 'scheme of things' must all be taken into account by practitioners in the field of vocational guidance.

Once an individual has selected a particular job, and an organization has selected and placed that individual, the organization is likely to employ appropriate training and development techniques in order to maximize the effectiveness of that individual in his job. It is to the subject of these training techniques that we now turn.

5
Training

One of the major reasons why people are trained, or retrained, is because the skills they possess are inappropriate to the task requirements of their jobs (see E3). Training programmes tend therefore to have fairly specific objectives, and education and training are frequently distinguished in terms of the degree of specificity of their aims. Both, however, depend upon a broad range of instructional techniques to promote effective learning and psychologists have been much concerned with the evaluation of such techniques in the laboratory, in industry and in the classroom. From this research, a number of general principles have emerged, although it is also clear that factors specific to the task to be learned, and characteristics of the individual learner, are of considerable importance.

Training is not the only way of attempting to correct a mismatch between the task requirements of jobs and the skills of individual operators, and selection procedures and work design also play a major role. The effectiveness of a training programme can be increased, for example, if individuals who are selected for participation possess the necessary aptitudes to develop the skills required. Furthermore, training is made easier if the tasks comprising the job for which the individual is to be trained are appropriately designed. Men can be trained to operate poorly designed systems, but there is an increased likelihood of errors occurring under conditions of increased work load, and, more particularly, in emergency situations.

Skilled performance

The concept of skill is central to the psychology of training. Skills are of many kinds, including physical, social, linguistic and intellectual. From the point of view of the task requirements of many industrial jobs, the perceptual and motor skills involved in sensori-motor performance are the most important (see A5); while the development of various social skills is becoming an increasingly important part of managerial training programmes.

Up until the 1940s, research on the acquisition of skills was relatively neglected. When skills were considered at all, they tended to be regarded as similar to 'habits' (Oldfield, 1959). However, the military, industrial and economic pressures of the Second World War necessitated much research and development of training procedures for the acquisition of skills. This was because the large increase in the size of the armed forces and the allocation of greater manpower to the manufacturing industries resulted in a number of individuals being faced with new jobs demanding new skills, which had to be rapidly mastered. It soon became clear that the principles stemming from research on learning were inadequate, since the kinds of laboratory tasks studied up to that time, such as reaction time and the memorization of nonsense syllables, provided completely inappropriate models for the skills involved in such tasks as operating a lathe, handling a tank or flying an aeroplane. As Bartlett (1951) expressed it: 'There was a process of gradually accumulating discontent with the classical methods of the experimental psychologists in a good many areas of investigation'. Psychologists, therefore, were forced to think afresh about the nature of skills, and somewhat different approaches to skilled performance gradually began to be adopted.

These were made possible by an increasing, and fruitful, collaboration between psychologists, physical scientists and engineers. During the Second World War, many new and highly complex weapons systems were devised. For the most part men had to operate these systems, and so psychologists were increasingly consulted about ways in which the performance of the system could be optimized. It gradually became apparent that this could only be achieved if the operators and the hardware were regarded as being a 'total system' and the concepts of the 'man-machine system' (referred to in Chapter 3) and the 'human operator' within it were developed (see E4).

The concept of the human operator developed by Craik (1948) used analogies both from cybernetics and from information theory. The human operator was considered to behave much like a class of self-regulating machines known as servomechanisms and to process information in accordance with the 'single channel hypothesis'. This hypothesis stated that there were bottlenecks in the chain of central mechanisms linking the sensory receptors to the motor effectors, which result in incoming information being recoded from parallel into serial form. As a result the human operator performing a sensori-motor task has a limited capacity for transmitting information in a given period of time. Thus the view of the operator that began to emerge resembled that shown in Figure 5.1 opposite.

Receptor processes involve the sensory systems of the body, such as the visual and auditory systems. Effector processes involve the muscles, tendons and joints, while translation processes refer to the central decision processes that intervene between sensory input and motor output, and include attentional, memory and response selection processes. Translation processes are essentially concerned with the choice of a response and it is to such processes that the single channel hypothesis is held to apply. When the operator performs a sensori-motor task, the sensory input is likely to come from a display and motor output is likely to result in the activation of a control. The two feedback loops convey to the operator the results of his actions. The internal feedback loop gives him kinaesthetic information (that is, information about his own movements). The external feedback loop provides information from the external environment, generally via the visual sense modality. Such information serves to tell the operator how closely his current attainment approximates to

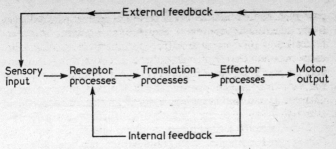

Fig. 5.1 *A simple model of the processes involved in the sensori-motor performance of the human operator*

the goal of some desired, or imposed, standard of performance.

As noted above, in performing a sensori-motor task, the operator is exercising to varying degrees his perceptual and motor skills. But skills have certain features in common and Welford (1958) suggests that all skills of whatever kind possess three main characteristics:

A. They consist essentially of the building of an organized and co-ordinated activity in relation to an object or situation and thus involve the whole chain of sensory, central and motor mechanisms which underlie performance.
B. They are learnt in that the understanding of the object or situation and the form of the action are built up gradually in the course of repeated experience.
C. They are serial in the sense that within the overall patterns of the skill many different processes or actions are ordered and co-ordinated in a temporal sequence. (p. 18)

How then do skills become acquired and how does the performance of the skilled operator differ from that of the unskilled? A general answer to the first question would seem to be, through practice and feedback, modified by training. Again, as Bartlett, cited by Welford (1968), put it, 'it is not practice, but practice *the results of which are known*, that makes perfect'.

A considerable body of evidence, reviewed by Annett (1969), dating from the earliest years of experimental psychology, has emphasized the necessity of providing feedback in the form of knowledge of the results of actions in order for learning to occur at all. But, as Annett and Kay (1957) point out, 'knowledge of results is not ... something which a scientist has ingeniously introduced into a training situation – it is something which will be inherent in that situation from the moment when the trainee is given any rudimentary idea as to what he is to try to do'. In utilizing knowledge of results as part of a training procedure, one of the trainer's main tasks becomes that of augmenting appropriately the feedback the trainee receives. This includes enabling the trainee to become aware of the intrinsic feedback the task itself provides.

Miller (1953) has distinguished between action and learning feedback, the first of which permits the operator to modify his ongoing response, that is, to guide his actions, while the second permits him only to modify the next. Thus action feedback is concurrent while learning feedback is delayed. As Holding (1965) points out, 'action feedback is not really knowledge of results, it is knowledge of the changing state of our attempts to produce results'. Action feedback generally produces fairly rapid increments in performance but, if it is withdrawn, performance declines markedly and abruptly. Since learning feedback compels the operator to rely much more on intrinsic cues, it produces both a slower rate of improvement and a slower and less marked rate of decline. Furthermore, any delay in obtaining concurrent feedback, through for example a control-display lag, is likely to disrupt skill acquisition, although with terminal feedback, delay has much less adverse effects. Feedback can also be immediate or delayed, non-verbal or verbal, continuous or intermittent and separate or accumulated (Holding, 1965). Thus, feedback can be given immediately after performance has terminated or a delay can be interposed; feedback can be provided non-verbally, for example, by a light or a buzzer, or verbally in the form of comments on the trainee's performance or by assigning him a performance score; feedback may be provided after every trial or only intermittently after occasional trials; finally, it can be accumulated over a series of trials. There are thus several kinds of feedback and that which is most appropriate in a particular situation differs in accordance with, and is sometimes constrained by, the specific skill being learned. Furthermore, different trainees appear to use feedback in different ways.

Turning to the second question posed above, there appear to be three main ways in which the performance of the skilled operator differs from that of the unskilled. On the receptor side, the information the operator receives becomes increasingly redundant. That is, he requires less information from the display to guide his performance and is also better able to anticipate future events, and thus improve his speed of performance. On the effector side, too, his performance is characterized by an increased economy of action. Finally, the timing of the whole sequence of actions involved in the skill becomes smoother and more coordinated. Thus, with practice, the perceptual and motor components of the skill begin to overlap temporally and hence become integrated. Good timing is the last element of skilled performance to be acquired.

In addition to the intrinsic feedback from the task itself, and the extrinsic feedback from the results of his own actions, the operator requires a clear understanding of the task and of the objectives of the man-task combination. A lack of appreciation of the nature of the skill to be acquired can clearly impede learning. A number of guidance methods, including charts and diagrams, films and demonstrations, have therefore been utilized in order to aid trainees to gain an understanding of the tasks they are to perform. A further example is magnification, which has been shown to exert beneficial effects on the acquisition of certain perceptual skills in the textile industry (Belbin, Belbin and Hill, 1957). Belbin *et al* used specially produced large-weave cloth in order to enable trainees for a job involving invisible mending to develop an understanding of the way in which the weave pattern was constructed. This resulted in training time being reduced from several months to a few weeks.

Research on the development of skills has also examined whether the different components of a task should be practised together, or in isolation, or built up in progressively larger combinations. Seymour (1956) compared the effectiveness of these three methods, known as the 'whole' method, the 'isolation' method and the 'progressive part' method, in training capstan lathe operators. In this study the progressive part and isolation methods produced better performance after five days of training. Similar results have been obtained with shoe machinists (Singleton, 1959) and post-office sorters (Belbin, 1964). Thus, where the task can be divided into component activities, the progressive part method seems to be beneficial. However, when this is impossible because the components of the skill involved are too closely interwoven, as for example in driving, the whole method is superior. The relative effectiveness of active and passive (or non-participation) methods has also been compared. The conclusion appears to be that both are important. As noted above, non-participation methods, such as films and demonstrations, can be useful in providing the operator with an understanding of the nature of the task. However, they need to be supplemented by active methods which enable intrinsic and extrinsic feedback to be utilized if the skill is to be developed successfully.

Training procedures

Training programmes are required when the probability of adequate performance without training is low and the costs of inadequate performance are high. Thus, the general objective of a training programme is to raise the performance of a specified population of trainees to a specified criterion level; the specific objectives depend both upon the characteristics of the job and those of the trainees. The form that a particular training procedure takes demands therefore an analysis of the characteristics of the job and an appraisal of the skill level of the target population. A decision concerning how the training programme is to be evaluated also needs to be made. Job analysis involves the description and specification of the task requirements of the job, while the appraisal of the skill level of the target population entails either an evaluation of the present level of job proficiency, if this is appropriate, or an assessment of relevant aptitudes and abilities. Thus, job analysis specifies the kind of operator required and skill appraisal enables the disparity between current and criterion performance to be estimated.

Training procedures can be divided into two broad categories: on-line or on-site training and off-line training. The former category includes 'on-the-job' training (sometimes termed 'sitting by Nellie'), coaching schemes and job rotation. Procedures in the latter category make use of training devices, such as programmed and computer-assisted instruction, simulators and business games as well as some of the non-participation methods mentioned earlier such as films or lectures. 'Sensitivity training', or T-group methods, can also be included in the category of off-line training techniques.

Although on-line training is probably more widespread, and has the advantage that transfer of learning (see A3) from the training situation to the job situation is maximized, it is often likely to be 'casual, unsystematic and poorly planned' (Bass and Barrett, 1972). Off-line training, on the other hand, can be less expensive, particularly if the job involves the use of expensive materials, and is frequently less hazardous. Furthermore, if a trainee operator is trained 'on the job' then there is inevitably a conflict between training and operational requirements. Off-line training permits the operator's proficiency to be assessed by stages, using tasks graded in difficulty and at the same time relevant to the skills being acquired. In this way the operator's exposure to the different aspects of the job can be optimized. We now turn to a brief consideration of some off-line training techniques.

Off-line training techniques

Programmed and computer assisted instruction

Programmed instruction is provided either by automated teaching devices or 'teaching machines' or by programmed manuals or textbooks. The information to be learned is organized by the programmer and divided into a large number of steps, or 'frames', progressing in a logical sequence from easy to difficult. Programmes can be described as linear or branching, and constructed-response or multiple choice. In a linear programme, the learner proceeds through the programme in an unbroken series of steps, whereas in a branching programme, he can be re-routed in order to obtain supplementary information. In a constructed-response programme, the individual has to compose his own answer to a problem, while in a multiple-choice programme he selects an answer from a list that is provided. The trainee operates the programme himself, proceeding at his own pace. At each step, he is posed a question based on the immediately preceding information and, depending upon whether his answer is correct or incorrect, he either continues through the programme or goes back to relearn the material wrongly dealt with. Thus, in programmed instruction, the trainee actively participates in learning, works at his own rate, handles only discrete items of information and obtains immediate knowledge of his progress.

In the late 1950s, a number of American companies began research programmes comparing the effectiveness of programmed instruction and the lecture method with respect to the acquisition of factual information. In general, these studies showed that learning time could be significantly reduced by programmed instruction, although the amount of information subsequently retained was not necessarily greater with this method. The best results appear to have been obtained with the learning of drills, rules and operating procedures, and applications include micrometer reading, equipment maintenance and sorting and inspection (Taylor, 1964). Programmed instruction has also been shown to be useful in the acquisition of some manual skills. Although much factual and some conceptual information can be acquired as, if not more, effectively in less time by means of programmed instruction (Leib *et al*, 1967), it is probably inappropriate for many aspects of managerial training involving, for instance, 'human relations' skills. Furthermore, as Bass and Barrett (1972) point out, the implementation of programmed instruction as a training procedure is initially expensive and requires painstaking development. They suggest, therefore, that only its use with large numbers of trainees over a long period is likely to justify its cost.

Programmed instruction can also be effected through the use of digital computers, although perhaps the major use of computer-assisted instruction is in 'adaptive training' where the computer automatically adjusts the difficulty level of the task being learned in accordance with the trainee's rate of progress. Adaptive training has been shown to be extremely effective in the learning of many complex perceptual-motor skills. Since large numbers of trainees can be linked to the computer at the same time, this technique, although again expensive, has clear advantages over conventional methods of instruction. But as with programmed instruction, the economic justification for computer-assisted instruction depends largely upon the extent to which it is used as part of a training programme.

Simulators and games

Simulators are simplified versions of a whole task, as in flying and driving simulators, or of some particular aspect of it. In the latter case, the trainee is able to practise a particularly difficult or complex part of the task away from the real task situation. Simulation techniques are clearly of value in situations where the real task is extremely expensive to operate, where unskilled behaviour is hazardous to the operator or to others, or where real conditions are unobtainable (e.g. in the case of simulated flights by space vehicles).

Many experiments concerned with 'transfer of training' between two tasks have shown that the degree of similarity between the two tasks is an important variable (Holding, 1965). Thus, a problem faced by simulator training is the degree of similarity or fidelity to real-task conditions that the simulated task should possess. The similarity between real and simulated tasks can vary in three main ways: first, in terms of the equipment, such as controls and displays, that is used in the two task situations; second, in terms of the environmental conditions under which the real task may be carried out and whether an attempt is made to simulate such conditions over a wide range, which is particularly important in the case of flying simulators; and third, in terms of the perceived similarity of the two task situations to the trainee. The cost of increasing the similarity of the two situations can often be considerable. Further it has been suggested that the relationship between the amount of performance transfer from a simulated to a real task and the degree of similarity of the two tasks may not be linear (Miller, 1954). Consequently, the question of how much fidelity to the real task situation the simulator needs to have has frequently been investigated.

In general, the answer seems to be the greater the fidelity, the greater is the positive transfer obtained, but 'how much more of what type of fidelity?' appears to be a question requiring close investigation in the particular circumstances of the training programme. Nevertheless, simulators have been shown to be useful training devices for a number of highly complex skills.

Business games can also be considered to simulate real situations, and since the mid-1950s a number of such games have been developed for use in management training situations. Many business games, which may last for several days, aim at training managers to make appropriate decisions concerning, for instance, financial policy or industrial relations. Individuals compete, either individually or in teams, against each other or against a computer. The state of play, usually expressed in terms of company profit or loss, is shown periodically in order to provide knowledge of the results of decisions. Such games appear to engender a high degree of involvement among the participants, but their effectiveness, in terms of achieving training objectives, is often questionable (Bass and Vaughan, 1966).

Lectures and films

Although the lecture method is an economical means of communicating information to a large number of trainees, it has many disadvantages. The lecture does not permit trainees to learn at their own pace, and even competent lecturers may not enable trainees to learn as effectively as textbooks or manuals. As with programmed instruction, films often permit the optimal use to be made of the best instructors available, and if such presentations are followed by discussion groups, then effective learning can often be promoted. Pictorial information is also of especial benefit in bringing about both a clear understanding of task objectives and in helping trainees with difficult aspects of the task to be learned.

Visual aids

Visual aids have been used in conjunction with training in the development of perceptual skills. An example of the use of these aids, which appears to have produced a dramatic improvement, is given by Chaney and Teel (1967). These investigators developed a set of visual aids in conjunction with a training programme designed to improve the performance of machine-parts inspectors. This job involved the examination of precision machined parts for such 'objective defects' as 'mislocated holes, threaded holes, lack of parallelism and concentricity, and improper dimensions' as well as for 'subjective defects' such as poor finish, scratches and nicks. Objective defects accounted for the majority of faults normally reported.

Chaney and Teel used a number of visual aids consisting of simplified drawings showing which features of the machined-parts were to be inspected and the tolerance limits for each objective defect. In addition, a training programme consisting of four one-hour sessions, and including lectures, demonstrations and questions, was employed. Comparisons were made between the effects of visual aids alone, training alone, or visual aids in conjunction with training on the detection of objective defects and the performance of a control group who received neither training nor visual aids. The control group showed a slight decline but all three treatment groups improved; the training alone group by 32 per cent, the visual aids alone group by 42 per cent and the combined group by 71 per cent. Clearly, then, in this study at least, the effects of the two procedures summate, although it is less apparent whether such effects are long-lasting.

Sensitivity training
Sensitivity or T-group training is a technique whose purpose is to increase the individual's skills in working with others (Smith, 1969) and the T-group method has been frequently used in the training and development of managers. The T-group is normally a small, unstructured, face-to-face group consisting of between 10 and 20 people. A trainer may be present but generally has no directing role. The participants of the T-group are encouraged to discuss the way in which they perceive themselves both generally and in relation to the rest of the group. The emphasis is upon the 'here and now' rather than upon past or possible future experiences. The technique is frequently alleged to inculcate an increased self-

awareness and an insight into the way the individual projects himself to others, as well as an increased sensitivity to the behaviour of others and the social cues they emit. The understanding of the way in which groups function and of the processes that enable groups to function successfully is thought to be enhanced. Finally, the T-group experience is sometimes supposed to result in a heightened ability to diagnose and remedy conflict situations within social groups (Campbell and Dunnette, 1968). Thus, the trainee in a T-group is often considered to acquire from the experience a general appreciation of the reasons why members of a social group act as they do, and a more specific understanding of the way in which he, as an individual, normally projects himself upon others, and of the effect of such behaviour.

Campbell and Dunnette (1968), in their review of the effectiveness of T-group experiences in management training and development, cautiously conclude that T-groups have been reasonably successful in inducing behavioural changes which persist when the manager returns to his organization. However, the nature of these changes has been difficult to specify. Some evidence suggests that a number of the aims of T-group training have been achieved in many studies, although the evaluation criteria seem in some cases to be suspect. Many of these criteria are internal, depending largely upon the participant's own evaluation. Furthermore, even when using internal criteria, few comparisons have been made between the effectiveness of T-groups and those of other situations which might produce similar effects, such as participating in another kind of group experience, or merely completing a self-description form. When the success of T-groups has been evaluated in terms of external criteria, such as changes in job effectiveness, it appears that the T-group experience exerts little effect.

Trainee characteristics

As mentioned earlier in this chapter, characteristics of the individual trainee can also influence the effectiveness of training procedures. The responsiveness of different trainees to the same training programme differs, and specialized training programmes may be required that are tailored to the needs of particular categories of trainee – for example, the older worker. A number of studies have indicated that, in general, the training needs of the older worker who is being retrained for a new job are somewhat different from those of younger workers (Belbin, 1964). In particular, older trainees must be allowed adequate time to master task objectives and should be prevented from making errors in the initial stages of training. In addition, the speed at which instruction is given should be under the control of the trainee, and the instruction should be related as directly as possible to the task to be learnt, with a minimum of intervening activity. Finally, the use of existing skills should be maximized. These general principles, of course, apply to a greater or lesser extent to all trainees but are of particular importance for the older trainee; and in a number of studies these general principles have been utilized to develop successful training procedures for the older worker.

Finally, the importance of organizational support in the success of training procedures should be mentioned. This again appears to be more important for some training groups than others. In the development and evaluation of a training programme for the hard-core unemployed, for example, Friedlander and Greenberg (1971) found that the organizational climate was the major determinant of the success of the programme. It is to more general aspects of the organizational setting that we now turn.

6
The organizational setting

This chapter is concerned with some of the factors associated with the satisfaction and performance of people at work, covering in more detail some of the points which were made in the last part of Chapter 1. It looks at three main topics. It is concerned with the motivation to work and seeks to explain why men and women work, why it is that some individuals work hard while others do as little as possible, or why some people seem to gain great satisfaction from work, while others express great distaste for it. Secondly it examines the part played by the behaviour of a manager or supervisor in determining the attitudes and behaviour of workers, and finally it looks at studies which have related aspects of organizational structure to organizational effectiveness and employee satisfaction.

The motivation to work

Since the end of the nineteenth century, the ideas of theorists on the motives of men at work have undergone dramatic changes. To Frederick W. Taylor and other advocates of 'scientific management' writing at this time, money was the prime motivating force. The 'scientific managers' were concerned by the problem of the time, which was how to achieve efficiency in large, technically complex factories, and propounded normative prescriptions (the 'one best way') to maximize productivity. The way to organize to achieve maximum efficiency was through the control of work, effective planning, a unity of command, clearly understood responsibilities, and so on. The organization was thus defined in terms of scientific principles used to describe the formal system. The key to organizational design was *span of control* (defined as the number of subordinates a manager is responsible for supervising) which created a system based on a centralized pyramidal authority structure. Underlying these and other prescriptions was a series of assumptions about the motivations of workers, based on the Calvinist work-ethic. The assumptions held that people inherently disliked work and that money was of prime importance in inducing men to work hard. Thus the worker had to be coerced into achieving work targets. He was also seen as lazy, lacking initiative and as unwilling to accept responsibility. Time and method studies were worked out to integrate these properties of the worker with the properties of the job, so that the worker would use less energy and yield more work.

The Hawthorne studies

The work of Elton Mayo at the Hawthorne works of Western Electric in the USA in the 1930s reported by Roethlisberger and Dickson (1939) challenged some of the assumptions of scientific management, with its emphasis on the carrot-and-stick, and ushered in the 'human relations' movement. The studies emphasized the importance of social factors at work and the influence of informal group norms on satisfaction and productivity. Studies were designed to investigate the effect of various degrees of illumination, of rest pauses, and the length of the working day on the efficiency of workers assembling electrical components. No simple relationship was discovered. Rather, in some conditions such as the investigation of illumination level, productivity rose regardless of experimental changes, while other studies showed apparently haphazard changes in output with no obvious explanation. Follow-up experiments and interviews with the workers showed that informal social groups within the organization influenced individual attitudes and job performance. One aspect of the Hawthorne studies, for example, provided an early account of output restriction. Men in the Bank Wiring Observation Room were paid on a system of group piecework for the whole department so that each man's earnings were affected by the output of every other man in the department. Yet the observers noted that fast workers in the group were restricting their output to hold their production within the informal group standard.

The Hawthorne researchers have been subjected to many criticisms. Carey (1967) has argued that it is impossible to draw firm conclusions from the studies because of uncontrolled factors in the experimental design, and that the conclusions the experimenters drew from the findings neither follow from nor are supportable from their data. Yet the studies have been very influential. They led to the demise of economic man, motivated by monetary self-interest. Workers were shown not to be passive individuals responding to incentives or avoiding hard work as Taylor had suggested but *groups* of workers establishing informal group norms for production. The men seemed to establish their identity in the group and were more responsive to the social pressures of their group than to the control of management. But while the Hawthorne work was an advance on the scientific management view, it too is certainly not a complete view. Many individuals seem to care nothing for the group standard or the ostracism of their colleagues. These 'rate-busters' defy group standards and produce far more than the average. The work of Maslow and Herzberg has emphasized these individual differences to a greater extent than Mayo.

Maslow
Maslow (1943) specified a need hierarchy common to all normal people and consisting, in ascending order, of physiological needs for air, food and water, safety needs, social needs, self-esteem or ego needs, and self-actualization needs. He argues that the lowest-level unsatisfied needs are the basic motivators of man. Thus, only when the physiological needs are satisfied will the next higher needs be the motivating factors of the individual. When that need is satisfied it no longer serves to motivate behaviour and the next higher need in the

hierarchy emerges. Maslow postulated that all human activity is an attempt to work upwards in the hierarchy towards the top need of self-actualization, the need of the individual to fulfil his potential.

However, when Maslow's formulations have been tested, the empirical results have not been clearly supportive. The question of whether physiological, safety, social, ego and self-actualization needs are separate and distinct is in some doubt. Some factor analytic studies have failed to find groupings of items which correspond to the Maslow categories. Other studies show that higher level needs may be related to job satisfaction even when lower level needs are not gratified, which is contrary to Maslow's postulations. Nevertheless, Maslow's work has greatly influenced the theories and research of others. A series of studies by Porter on the motivations of managers is based on ideas derived from Maslow's need hierarchy. Alderfer (1969) has proposed a theory which retains the hierarchical ordering but reduces the need hierarchy to three needs, existence, relatedness and growth needs, and describes how frustration of the higher order needs influences the lower order ones, a problem which is not considered by Maslow. Organizational theorists such as Argyris and McGregor have embraced Maslow's views and feel that it is in the best interest of the organization and of its members to structure the organization to permit the individual to achieve and satisfy his esteem, autonomy and self-actualization needs.

Herzberg

Herzberg is another theorist whose ideas have had a profound effect on the thinking of many people, especially among the business community. Herzberg *et al* (1959) and Maslow are alike in viewing the work itself as the source of true job satisfaction. According to Herzberg, good working conditions and satisfactory social relationships on the job can only serve to make the job tolerable.

Herzberg's Two Factor Theory rests principally on a detailed study of 200 engineers and accountants who were asked to recall those incidents in their job about which they felt exceptionally 'good' or 'bad' and to describe what happened. He found that the sources of satisfaction were very different from the sources of dissatisfaction. Good times at work were related to the job itself, such as achievement, recognition, responsibility and advancement. Bad times at work were the result of job *context* factors like pay, poor working conditions, security and interpersonal relations. Factors associated with the job itself were 'motivators' since they fulfilled the individual's need for self-actualization and growth, while the job context factors were 'hygiene factors' whose presence in the job merely prevented dissatisfaction. Only the satisfiers can provide the positive motivation to greater productivity. Putting effort into improving working conditions will only reduce or eliminate dissatisfaction according to the Two Factor Theory. Workers will only be persuaded to put in more effort if the work is designed to increase responsibility, improve recognition, and so on. This, of course, is the basis of job enlargement and enrichment programmes described in Chapter 3.

Many studies employing the critical incident methodology used by Herzberg have given essentially the same results across a variety of occupational groups. But studies employing different measures from those used by Herzberg have generally failed to support his findings. Many researchers are of the opinion that the results are bound by the critical incident interview technique which forces individuals to think in terms of a dichotomy. It is also probable that when people are asked to describe events that were satisfying to them, they tend to put themselves in the best light but when asked to describe bad times, defensive processes operate which encourage people to put the blame on others or on factors outside their control.

Equity theory
Basically, equity theory states that individuals employed by an organization want an equitable return for the contributions they make. People are said to compare the ratio of the inputs to the job to the outputs of the job and to examine how they match up. Inequity or imbalance in the ratio creates tension which is proportional to the magnitude of the inequity. The tension creates a drive to reduce the inequity. A number of studies designed to test the theory appear to support it. Sub-

jects working on various experimental tasks tended to decrease their output when they felt underpaid and to increase their performance when they felt overpaid. Subjects overpaid on an hourly rate of pay tended to increase the *quantity* of their work, while subjects overpaid on a piece rate basis decreased their output but increased the *quality* of their work, since feelings of inequity could only be reduced by low productivity. Thus, subjects hired on a piece rate basis for a proof-reading task who were led to believe that they were overpaid read fewer pages in one hour and detected more errors in the pages than other groups who felt more fairly paid (Adams and Jacobsen, 1964).

Equity theory is useful in providing explanations for certain phenomena which are otherwise hard to explain, but at present it is rather vague as a theory of motivation or satisfaction and there are some major issues which need clarification. The theory is based on the individual's view of his investments in, and rewards from, a relationship including that with an organization. But it is difficult to define which are the important variables in an industrial setting. Pay, promotions, interpersonal relationships, fringe benefits, status, or satisfaction with the work could all be considered rewards, or outputs, from work. A similar range of variables, including education, training, experience, age, loyalty and effort, can be conceived of as inputs. How a person actually goes about reducing inequity is also an interesting and important question which remains to be fully explored.

Expectancy theory

Vroom (1964) has proposed a cognitive model of motivation which attempts to explain motivation in the work environment. The key variables in Vroom's model are valence, expectancy and outcome. Valence refers to affective orientations toward particular outcomes, and outcomes can be positive or negative in valence. If an outcome has positive valence, this means that an individual would like to achieve it, while an outcome with negative valence is one that a person prefers not to attain. Thus, if a person works harder it may bring him more money (a positive valence) but may mean that he spends less time with his wife and children (negative valence).

101

Whether or not a person works harder depends on the *net* attractiveness of these and many other outcomes, with each outcome potentially having different amounts of positive or negative valence.

Expectancy is defined as a belief concerning the likelihood that a particular act will be followed by a particular outcome. An individual's motivation to carry out a particular act is a function of his expectancy and the strength of his valence.

Campbell *et al* (1970) suggest that there are two types of expectancy: the expectancy that successful performance is possible if effort is expended and the expectancy that successful performance will lead to an outcome. An example of the first type of expectancy would be the degree to which a sales manager expects that if he exerts greater effort he can increase sales by 10 per cent in one year. The second type of expectancy would be the degree to which he believes that he will be rewarded with promotion if he succeeds in increasing sales by 10 per cent.

Moreover, there are two classes of outcome. In the organizational setting, the first class of outcomes include such things as pay and promotion. These things have no value in themselves but are valuable in terms of their instrumental role in securing second level outcomes such as (hypothetically) food, clothing, housing, entertainment and status.

It can be seen that the theory is by no means easy to grasp. A simple example may help. Suppose a market gardener has a spare acre of land and is considering planting it with lettuces. Expectancy theory provides a framework for understanding the conditions under which he may or may not plant this extra acre. The factors determining this extra effort include the expectancy that the lettuces will grow to marketable size; the expectancy that he will make a profit if he does sell them; the attractiveness of this profit (positive valence) and the negative valences associated with tending lettuces on a cold, wet day; and the degree to which he believes the first level outcome (profit) will lead to the desired second level outcome of a colour television.

Many more outcomes can be conceived for a situation such as this. Expectancy theory assumes that an individual calculates the sum of the valence and probability index of each of these outcomes before acting. It also assumes that individuals behave rationally and logically in decision-making situations. In order for the psychologist to understand the determinants of the impulse to action he must perform a similar analysis of the expectancies and valences of outcomes as seen by the individual. This is obviously no easy task, and testing of the theory is still in its early stages.

Expectancy theory is an important step, however, in defining some of the variables which may operate to determine the effect of pay on the motivation to perform effectively, and strongly emphasises the importance of an individual's beliefs in the relationship between pay and performance. Lawler (1971) neatly summarizes some of the conditions that must prevail for pay to motivate good job performance:

1 Employees must attach a high positive valence to pay....
2 Employees must believe that good performance does in fact lead to high pay.
3 Employees must believe that the quality of their job performance reflects to a large extent how hard they are trying. In other words, they must feel that they can control the quality of their job performance. Unless this condition exists, employees will not believe that working hard will eventually lead to high pay.
4 Employees must see the positive outcomes tied to good performance as greater than the negative ones....
5 Employees must see good job performance as the most attractive of all possible behaviors. Only then will they be motivated to direct their effort toward performing well....
(p. 91)

Individual differences and the need for achievement

Many contributors to the field of motivation at work have highlighted the importance of individual differences. Korman (1970), for example, has indicated that individuals are motivated to perform in a manner which is consistent with their self-image. His studies suggest that only people with high self-esteem (i.e. people who believe themselves to be competent individuals) try to achieve ends which they see as desirable. Most satisfaction is derived from attainment in situations which are in balance with a person's self-perceptions.

McClelland (1961) has extensively studied differences between individuals in the need for achievement (n Ach), and suggests that the achievement motive is fairly consistent throughout a person's life. Individuals with higher than average need for achievement work longer and harder than others to accomplish a job and are less concerned with socializing with others than more socially-orientated individuals. But this only applies to tasks that will give them a feeling of accomplishment, which tend to be those of intermediate difficulty or of moderate risk. The high achiever is keen to obtain feedback on how well he is doing in the job, and such tasks yield more information about his capabilities than extremely hard or extremely easy tasks.

Similarly, individuals high on achievement motivation approach achievement-related activities and persist in them longer because they see success or failure as determined by their own efforts and thus experience greater internal rewards and punishments. They value money as a recognition for achievement, rather than for its own sake. Money is only an incentive to work hard for those with low achievement needs, not for those with high need for achievement. McClelland measures n Ach by means of a projective technique called the Thematic Apperception Test (TAT) in which subjects tell stories about the perceived content of a series of pictures. The stories are then analysed to reveal the amount of achievement motive expressed. The use of the TAT as a measure of n Ach has received criticism for its low test-retest reliability and its high sensitivity to the conditions of testing, but the concept of n Ach is a plausible one. McClelland reports, for example, that managers with high n Ach get more promotions and pay rises, are judged more effective and work for more successful firms than do managers with low n Ach. McClelland and his associates have also designed management development programmes to increase the need for achievement in individuals. They showed that those who underwent training subsequently had higher gross incomes and were more active in initiating new business activities, in capital investment and in stimulating business growth than those who did not. This type of entrepreneurial activity was particularly pronounced where the opportunity was greatest, i.e. where the individual was in fact in charge of the business.

Achievement motivation theory also links up with certain aspects of expectancy theory, since it can account for certain aspects of behaviour related to future outcomes. Thus Raynor (1970) found that American students with high n Ach earned higher exam grades when the grade was viewed as instrumental to career success than when it was not.

Management and supervisory styles

An individual's work motivation is not the only factor affecting his satisfaction and performance at a job. Organizations are usually arranged hierarchically, with a division of labour and a resulting need for co-ordination. Supervisors and managers play an important role in such co-ordination and are endowed with authority over their subordinates. Management or supervisory style refers to the way that the manager or supervisor exercises his authority and the general way in which he treats his subordinates. The behaviour of the immediate supervisor is a major force in determining the performance and satisfaction of those under him, and has been found to be related to labour turnover, absenteeism, accidents and grievances.

A series of studies conducted at the University of Michigan (Likert, 1961) was concerned with examining the managerial style of the 'good' and 'bad' departments in many different types of organization. The criteria for good and bad included productivity, absenteeism, turnover and employee motivation. The good departments were found to have supervisors who were 'employee-centred' while the poorer units had 'job-centred' supervisors.

The 'employee-centred' supervisor showed concern for his subordinates and considered their feelings. The 'job-centred' supervisor placed primary emphasis on production and directed group activities much more towards these ends than the employee-centred supervisor.

A similar large-scale research project was conducted at Ohio State University (Stogdill and Coons, 1957) which yielded similar results. A pool of about 1800 statements concerning supervisory behaviour was collected and, after preliminary analysis, reduced in number to form the Leader Behaviour Description questionnaire. Factor analyses of field surveys in different organizations reduced the items to two major clusters called 'consideration' and 'initiating structure', whose definitions followed closely those for employee-centred and job-centred supervisors.

The considerate supervisor is easy to approach, asks for subordinates' opinions on important matters, shows respect for their ideas, puts subordinates' suggestions into operation and gains their approval before going ahead. The considerate manager may also make use of participatory approaches, such as holding regular meetings with his subordinates. The directive, initiating manager, on the other hand, sees that subordinates are working to full capacity, maintains standards rigorously, emphasizes the meeting of deadlines, decides what should be done and how it should be done, criticizes subordinates in front of others, acts without consulting them, and generally shows more concern with the work than with the workers.

In the Ohio State research the two characteristics of consideration and initiating structure were found to be statistically independent dimensions (while 'employee-centredness' and 'job-centredness' were not said to be independent), such that a manager's score on one scale was independent of his score on the other. Generally, the most effective supervisors were those who scored high on both scales, while ineffective leaders were low on both.

Blake and Mouton (1964) have labelled the two dimensions 'concern for people' and 'concern for production'. Although concern for production is not identical with initiation of structure, it does tend to correlate fairly strongly with it. Blake and Mouton have devised a 'Managerial Grid' which makes it possible for a manager to analyse his own managerial style by use of two orthogonal nine-point scales, one for each variable, producing a grid of 81 squares. Nine on one scale shows high consideration for people, while nine on the other shows extreme concern for production. A score of one shows total lack of concern. The 'Managerial Grid' has been used on many management development programmes and has generally been found a useful means of conceptualizing the independence of the two dimensions and of examining the desirability of a manager's style moving towards the 9/9 square.

It is an indispensable first step to be able to describe managerial styles and to develop techniques for measuring them. It is an important second step to examine the effects of that behaviour on satisfaction and performance at work. The Ohio State studies noted that the most effective leaders were high on both consideration and initiating structure. Later studies by Fleishman and Harris (1962) indicate that there may be a curvilinear relationship between these supervisory characteristics and certain measures of employee dissatisfaction. These investigators asked subordinates to indicate (by means of the Leader Behaviour Description questionnaire) the extent to which they saw their foreman as considerate and as initiating structure. Foremen who were seen as considerate had lower grievance rates in their departments than those foremen who exhibited more initiation. Similarly, turnover was high with inconsiderate supervisors and low with considerate ones who exhibited less initiation. But beyond certain critical levels, increasing consideration or decreasing structure had no effect on grievance or turnover rates. Individual differences must also be brought into the picture. Not everyone wants democratic, participative leadership. A study by Sadler (1968) showed that although more employees preferred this style than any other, an authoritarian style was preferred by many employees.

Even if a participative style is more likely to produce satisfaction than an authoritarian one, does it also promote productivity and if so, under what conditions? Vroom (1962) showed that delivery men at twenty-seven stations were more likely to meet delivery quotas if they had participative supervisors, and many other surveys have indicated a similar relationship between a participative style and productivity. However, laboratory experiments have failed to consistently demonstrate the same results. One explanation for this, which is often given, is that it is not that participation in an industrial setting results in high productivity, but that supervisor consideration results *from* higher productivity and/or work satis-

107

faction. In other words, when productivity is high the supervisor can afford to be more participative and considerate since subordinates are working well. When productivity is low, the supervisor may feel he has to be more directive with his subordinates. Alternatively, both these influences may operate, with managers' behaviour affecting subordinates' attitudes and behaviour, and subordinates' attitudes and performance affecting managerial style.

While these alternative explanations may indeed be true, there is some longitudinal data to support the hypothesis that supervisory behaviour does affect performance. One study in the Michigan series cited earlier showed that managers in high-producing departments and those in low-producing departments who were exchanged, retained their former style towards their subordinates. But productivity did alter after the change-over of supervisors, with the low-producing departments improving and the high-producing departments deteriorating in productivity.

Nevertheless, it does seem that there is no simple relationship between supervisory behaviour and either worker satisfaction or performance. The proponents of participative management argue persuasively that everyone can participate in the decision process and should do so for the sake of satisfaction and productivity. There is accumulating argument and evidence that this view is an oversimplification. Which style a manager should adopt and which approach he is more inclined to use may depend on the manager's personal qualities, the attributes of his subordinates, the task to be performed, and the external environment of the organization. A few examples of the importance of these variables will serve to illustrate the point that there is no 'one best way'.

Fiedler's (1967) contingency theory of leadership, for example, states that the productivity of a group will depend on the extent to which the leader is esteemed. Groups are likely to be most productive under a task-oriented supervisor if he is either very little esteemed by his subordinates or very highly esteemed by them, whereas the same groups are likely to be most productive under a relationship-oriented supervisor of intermediate esteem or status.

The level in the organization of both superior and subordinate influences the superior's style. Higher level managers are dealing with educated, creative, high status subordinates who expect the opportunity to participate in the long-range problems of planning and policy with which such managers typically deal. At lower levels with more clearly defined objectives, shorter time scales, more structured tasks, and probably less educated subordinates, there may be fewer expectations to participate in decision-making.

The degree of authoritarian style exhibited by a supervisor depends on the extent to which subordinates are themselves authoritarian or prefer an authoritarian style (Vroom, 1960) and the achievement motivation of group members affects which leadership style is likely to be most effective. Misumi and Seki (1971) found that groups constituted of individuals with high n Ach were most effective when the leader emphasized both performance and group maintenance, while in low n Ach groups a strongly performance-oriented style was most effective.

Finally, work-unit size and the geographical location of the organization affects supervisor behaviour and subordinate preferences. The acceptability of authoritarian supervisory behaviour is greater in large units than small units, while cross-cultural studies have shown that managers from some countries (including the USA and Britain) prefer participative to directive approaches, while managers from other countries (such as India and Greece) prefer directive approaches.

Organization structure

The first part of this chapter examined the broad question of why men work and the second part has looked at why certain of these individuals, supervisors and managers, act the way they do. These two questions are interdependent. The behaviour of supervisors can increase or decrease the satisfaction of workers with their jobs by, for example, providing the opportunity for individuals to satisfy their desire for self-actualization or contact with others. But the extent to which a supervisor can be participative or directive, and the extent to which he can affect subordinates' motivation through facilitation or blocking of value attainment, are limited by the organizational system in which they all must work. This section will briefly examine some of the organizational variables which affect employee satisfaction and productivity. But first, it will examine efforts that have been made to understand the organization, since to describe how different aspects of an organization affect the attitudes and behaviour of individuals relies on careful descriptions of organizations themselves.

Some of the earlier approaches have already been described, including the economic and engineering theories about man and organizations exemplified by Taylor, theories concerning 'social man' and the human relations approach, and theories of 'self-actualizing man' with its emphasis on job enlargement. Current theorists have built on the strengths and weaknesses of the previous approaches and tend to see man as complex and motivated by many things. They emphasize individual differences, pointing out that men have different needs and goals. So it is with organizations. Organization theorists emphasize the conditions under which one type of organization is more effective than another, and conceive of organizations as open social systems. The system is open to the outside environment. It receives inputs of energy, materials, men and information from the outside world, processes these inputs, and provides outputs of goods, services, profits, and benefits for the employees, such as job satisfaction. The organization attempts all the while to reduce uncertainty, or increase predictability, and searches for ways to maintain control over the process. These theories emphasize how forces in the environment interact with and modify the organization and they avoid the general prescriptions which characterized earlier approaches.

Among the attempts to establish typologies of organization in the last twenty years has been the work of Woodward, and Pugh and his colleagues. Joan Woodward (1965) has shown that organizations can be usefully described on the basis of the production technology employed. Work by Pugh *et al* (1969) has established an empirical taxonomy of organizations composed of three factors: the structuring of activities (the degree of specialization, formalization of procedures, etc), the concentration of authority (the extent to which decision-taking is concentrated at the top), and line control of workflow (the degree to which control is exercised by line personnel as distinct from its exercise through impersonal procedures). Many of these fundamental attributes of an organization determine its effectiveness, as well as member satisfaction and performance, and a brief examination of what is known about this relationship follows.

Technology
A study by Woodward (1965) has added greatly to our knowledge concerning the extent to which production technology determines an organization's structure and suggests that there is a pattern of organization appropriate to the technology employed. The firms in Woodward's sample were divided into a ten-category scale of production technology complexity. These ten categories fell into three large technological divisions (with some slight overlap): small batch and unit production (e.g. production of unique units to customer's orders), large batch and mass production (e.g. assembly line techniques) and process production (e.g. production of chemicals by continuous processing). In unit production the production technology was fairly simple, while process production required a highly integrated, automated production system. Mass production was intermediate in complexity.

As the production technology became more complex, so the proportion of managers, clerical and supervisory staff to other personnel increased. The number of levels of authority in the management hierarchy also increased. Process production featured smaller spans of control with taller hierarchies of four to eight levels. Unit production had the flattest structures, with two to four levels and much wider spans of control. Decision-making was more centralized and directive in those companies involved in mass or batch production while in continuous process industries decisions were more likely to be made in committees with considerable participation. Specialization of function in management was found more frequently in batch and mass production firms. In unit production there were few specialists, while in process firms the line managers were also technical specialists. Concerning employee satisfaction, Woodward suggests that the employees had higher morale in unit production and in process production than in mass production technologies, which accords with other research mentioned in Chapter 3.

Similar in some respects to the influential study by Woodward is work by Burns and Stalker (1961). These authors investigated a number of manufacturing organizations including electronics firms, in which the technology and the market were changing fast, and a firm producing rayon with a process production and a relatively stable market. A flexible, 'organismic' system with, for example, a lack of well-defined job roles and with authority vested in the person who can most appropriately deal with the immediate problem was most appropriate to firms with rapidly changing objectives and technology. A more formal, 'mechanistic' kind of organization with a great division of labour, clear hierarchy of authority and centralized decision-making was most appropriate where the objectives and technology were well established and not subject to change. Some of the electronics firms who attempted to use a mechanistic structure were in severe difficulties.

Organizational climate

The 'climate' of the organization is another factor which can affect employee satisfaction and organizational performance. The term 'organizational climate' has been used in different ways by different investigators but is most usefully reserved to describe conditions inside the organization but outside the immediate face-to-face working group. It includes perceived attributes of the work environment, determined by management, and organizational practices that affect the motivation and behaviour of employees. Questionnaires have been designed to assess organizational climate and measure four main features: the degree of autonomy allowed to employees, the degree of structure, the rewards and punishments that affect worker attitudes and performance, and the degree of consideration, warmth and support provided.

Advocates of the participative approach to management argue that satisfaction and productivity will be greater with less structure. Likert (1967) does provide some support for this view by showing that organizations that change towards a less structured, complex and formal organization are more productive and have improved morale, but suggests that it may take a very long while for these positive results to follow from the changes. Moreover, once again it is probable that the relation between less structure and more productivity may depend, among other things, on the task to be performed.

Size

As organizations become larger, so the capacity of individuals to form relations with others becomes exhausted. Subgroups form within the larger organization, which increases the chance of conflict between the subgroup and the larger organization, and between subgroups. Larger organizations tend to be more bureaucratic, with more mechanistic organization processes such as communication and co-ordination and with more job specialization. This leads to decreases in worker satisfaction, in opportunities to participate in decisions which affect himself, in identification with the goals of the larger organization and in the amount of intrinsic job satisfaction derived by the organization members. Increases in worker dissatisfaction are associated with such behavioural indices as increased turnover, absenteeism, lateness and labour disputes. The relationship between size and accidents, and size and productivity is less clear cut.

One question which has not been satisfactorily answered is whether these indices of blue collar worker morale are associated with the size of the total organization or with subunits within the larger organization, since some investigators have taken total organization as their subject of study while others have taken subunits within the organization. Porter and Lawler (1965) noted that the evidence is stronger for an association between worker satisfaction and subunit size, rather than satisfaction and total organization size. This suggests that studies which confirm the negative consequences of total organization size may merely have sampled organizations with larger subunit size, or that there is a correlation between total organization size and subunit size.

As far as managers are concerned, Porter (1963) has shown that the effect of size is modified by managerial level. In relatively small companies, managers at lower and middle levels were more satisfied than managers at the same level in large companies. But the reverse was true at top levels of management.

Many other aspects of organization structure have an impact on employee attitudes and behaviour. A good review of empirical work in this field is provided by Porter and Lawler (1965). Apart from the variables of subunit and total organization size examined here, their review suggests that:

1 Job satisfaction increases with increasing levels in the organization. This relationship holds not only from rank-and-file positions to managerial positions but also from lower management positions to middle- and upper-level positions. Need satisfaction increases directly as level in the hierarchy increases, with the most significant increases in those areas of work which satisfy needs for self-actualization. Level also affects the behaviour exhibited by employees. The amount of information a person receives, the types of interpersonal relationships he has on the job and the types and nature of the decisions he must make in his position are affected by his level, especially within managerial ranks.

2 The distinction between line and staff positions affects satisfaction. Traditionally, positions in the line hierarchy have been within the direct chain of command and concerned with the main operations of the organization, while staff's function is advisory and involves providing specialized aid to the line (e.g. it includes personnel, work study, quality control and accountancy). The review shows that staff managers derive less satisfaction from their jobs than line managers.

3 Organization size affects the relative advantage of tall and flat organization structures. A flat organization structure is one where there are few levels relative to the total size of the organization and a tall organization structure is one where there are many levels relative to the total size of the organization. It appears that in relatively small organizations a flat structure is advantageous in terms of producing managerial job satisfaction, while in larger organizations a

114

tall structure is better in terms of satisfaction and productivity.

4 No firm conclusions could be reached as to the effects of the structural properties of centralized/decentralized shape and span of control.

7
The older worker

This chapter is concerned with some of the employment and retirement problems faced by older workers. The former apply mainly to blue-collar workers, though white-collar workers are not immune from their effects. As noted in Chapter 1, demographic changes have resulted in a marked increase in the sheer numbers of older people in the populations of most industrial societies, and rapid technological advance has frequently rendered obsolescent many of the work-related skills and qualifications which the present older generation acquired early in life. In addition, although there has been an increasing social awareness of, and general public sympathy for, the plight of many old-age pensioners, it seems likely that at the same time the status and satisfactions of the majority of older individuals, relative to those of younger people, have undergone a decline in most industrial societies.

In an examination of anthropological evidence bearing on the position of the aged in a number of countries, Palmore (1971) suggested that the status and security of the aged reached a peak in highly developed agricultural societies. However, much of the respect and power, derived from their control of productive property and also from their store of knowledge and experience, that accrued to older persons in stable agrarian societies has been swept away in the transition to an industrial society. Industrial societies also provide fewer opportunities for the old to carry out auxiliary, but nevertheless socially useful, tasks. In consequence, older people must either take their chance in the labour market where, by and large, they often fare rather badly, or live in retirement. There they face conditions of relative economic deprivation (compared to the younger and more productive members of society), a situation which further weakens their status.

The transition from a predominantly agricultural to a predominantly industrial society has the effect of reducing the labour force participation rates of elderly people. R. M. Belbin and Clarke (1971), using data for 1960 or thereabouts taken from the United Nations compendium of social statistics for 1967, compared the percentages of men aged 65 and over employed in fourteen agricultural and seventeen industrial countries, an industrial country being defined as one in which less than 25 per cent of the labour force were employed in agriculture. Computing means from the data they compiled, it appears that, on average, 57 per cent of men over 65 were employed in agricultural countries but only 30 per cent in industrial countries. Earlier data concerning the employment of men over 65, for about 1950, suggest figures of 37.7 per cent for 21 industrialized countries, 61 per cent for 30 semi-industrialized countries and 70.1 per cent for 21 agricultural countries.

In advanced industrial countries, for example, the United States, there has also been a long-term trend, dating from the last decades of the nineteenth century, towards progressively earlier retirement. The labour force participation rate of American men aged 65 and over has thus declined from 68.3 per cent in 1890 to 27.8 per cent in 1965. This long-term decline in the employment of elderly men has not been accompanied by any overall reduction in the size of the American labour force however, and it appears that the reduced participation of older men has been counterbalanced by the increased participation of women aged 45 to 64. This rose from 12.1 per cent in 1890 to 46.6 per cent in 1965 (Odell, 1970). Nevertheless, because of greater longevity and better health, the average length of an American's working life has increased from 31 years in 1900 to 42 years in 1966 (Kimmel, 1974). Furthermore, largely through technological advances, the productivity of the American labour force has been vastly increased. Hence, it has been argued (although not conclusively) that there is an adequate supply of manpower to meet existing demands for goods and services, even without the participation of older men; and an implication of this argument is that the continuance of older men in the work force increases the threat of unemployment for, and perhaps weakens the bargaining power of, younger ones.

Some American labour unions, notably the car workers and the steelworkers, have responded to this implication by negotiating early retirement schemes on behalf of their members (Gordon, 1970). In some cases such schemes permit a man to retire, with a reduced pension, as early as 58, as well as, incidentally, helping to make more jobs available for younger workers. Gordon also notes a trend towards decreasing labour force participation among non-white males in the age range 45 to 64, which suggests that age barriers to employment are moving further downwards than has previously been the case. It thus appears that in the USA, where the problems faced by older workers have perhaps received more extensive investigation than they have elsewhere, there are strong pressures operating whose effect is to reduce participation in the labour force by older men, although, apparently, these pressures are not operating as strongly in the case of older women (Sweet, 1973). Similar trends are discernible in most other industrialized societies.

While the *extent* of unemployment among older age groups up to age 65 may not be markedly different from that of younger age groups, the older worker in most industrialized countries appears to bear the greater brunt of *long-term* unemployment. In the United States in the late 1960s, 20 per cent of the total unemployed and 40 per cent of the long-term unemployed (defined as a period of twenty-seven weeks or more) were aged 45 or over. At around the same time in the United Kingdom, men over 55 years of age, on becoming unemployed, were likely to remain so for four times as long as those under 25.

But even before retirement, the kind of employment in which many older workers are typically found undergoes fairly marked changes. Sobel (1970), in an examination of the impact of economic and technological change upon older worker utilization patterns that has taken place in the United States since 1930, points out that the occupational and labour force profile of older workers is significantly different from that of younger workers. Older men are found, in disproportionate numbers, in many unskilled service occupations which require low levels of skill and training. Sobel notes that in many cases these represent the only areas of employment in which older workers, displaced from more highly paid jobs requiring high levels of skill, can readily find work without encountering age discrimination in the form of age-related hiring limits. There is also a predominance of older workers in declining industries such as mining, textiles and the railways, where employment opportunities have declined in absolute terms, as well as in industries such as steel, where the rate of growth of employment opportunities has risen more slowly than the size of the labour force as a whole. A further category of employment where older workers are to be found in large numbers are 'low level and menial service fields' and in industries manufacturing non-durable goods. Finally, on the credit side, many of the traditional professions, such as pharmacists, physicians and surgeons, dentists and lawyers and judges, contain large numbers of older men. However in these areas too the rate of employment increase has apparently been well below the United States national average for professional workers. As already implied, the problems faced by the older American worker are probably more severe than are those faced by older workers in other countries. However, at the international colloquium in which Sobel's analysis was presented, the discussion of his paper concluded by expressing the view that although the older worker problem is somewhat different in most European countries, employment trends and problems are 'very much the same only not yet as acute'.

In the light of the age discrimination that many older workers clearly experience, various efforts have been made to improve the position of the older worker through legislation. In the United States, attempts to minimize the vulnerability of the older worker in the labour market culminated in the passage of the Age Discrimination in Employment Act of 1967. Prior to the passage of the Act, the United States Department of Labour made a study of age discrimination in employment, together with its economic and personal consequences (Grunewald, 1972). The personal consequences can well be imagined. Concerning economic consequences the study found that the unemployment of older workers was costing the American economy 'an estimated *one million man years of productive time annually*' (Grunewald, 1972, our italics). The Age Discrimination in Employment Act of 1967 covers workers aged between 40 and 65 in an estimated 685,000 establishments employing 43m people (about 50 per cent of the work force) and prohibits discrimination in employment because of age in matters of hiring, job retention and compensation, as well as in other conditions or privileges of employment. Up to now no legislation against occupational discrimination has been passed in Britain, although an 'Age Level of Employment Bill', sponsored by Edward Milne, then M.P. for Blyth, was proposed in 1971. However, the 1968 revision of the 1965 Redundancy Payments Act, designed to encourage employers, when dismissals are inevitable, to lay off younger workers before dismissing older workers, appears to have had some beneficial effects on the unemployment rate for older workers (Slater, 1972). It is probable that such legislation will produce some short-term amelioration of the position of the older worker, although in the longer term, the outlook is less certain.

Given that older workers remain a source of valuable manpower in most economies, that their employment results in an increase in consumer spending, as well as producing increased tax revenues, while their unemployment raises charges on public assistance and welfare services, why do they fare less well in the labour market? There are probably four main answers to this question. First, older workers are generally much less mobile than younger ones and are usually unwilling to be uprooted from their communities in order to find employment elsewhere. Secondly, they are, on the whole, less willing to take advantage of retraining schemes when these are provided. The third and fourth answers emphasize respectively economic factors and the prevailing stereotype of the older worker. The costs of hiring older workers are sometimes thought to be high. Fjerstad (1965), in a study of the economic considerations to be taken into account when hiring older workers, found that it was slightly more expensive to do so, principally because of the increased cost of pensions and of accident and sickness insurance. However, these increased costs were largely compensated for by improvements in absenteeism, turnover, accident-rates and productivity.

The importance of the prevailing stereotype of the older worker has been clearly expressed by Stagner (1971), who argues that the employment problems of older workers are largely attributable to the stereotypes of this group held by employers and younger employees.

He remarks, 'the social impact of this stereotype is greatest when it is held by an employer, but it is also widespread among older workers themselves, and – regrettably – even among gerontologists'.

Older workers are frequently assumed to be deficient in a number of respects, ranging from physical and mental skills to temperamental and personality factors. Clearly, changes take place with age in a variety of characteristics (Bromley, 1974) but it remains to be demonstrated that these characteristics are related to successful job performance or to satisfaction with work, and also that they are independent of the effects of stereotyping. Where changes relevant to job performance can be shown to occur, the problem becomes one of minimizing the importance of such changes through counselling and retraining procedures and, sometimes, through job redesign. As Stagner emphasizes, it thus becomes important to think of any worker, whether or not he is over the age of 45, as an individual whose skills and social qualities should be individually assessed.

Stagner further observes, 'It seems to me that, in so far as employment of the older worker is a matter of concern, it must be a concern of all industrial psychologists and personnel men. There are not any new principles of perception, learning, motivation or thinking which have unique relevance to people past 45, or past 65. The methods of personnel selection, training, orientation and leadership which apply to young worker populations apply also to older workers. The hub of the problem is not the change in the worker, but the change in the way he is perceived by employers, foremen, and fellow employees'. He therefore sees the main task for psychologists interested in the problems of the older worker as being to break down these stereotypes, although he admits that this will be extremely difficult.

To what extent is there a rational basis for this stereotype of the older worker? We have mentioned earlier that there is much reliable evidence which contradicts it, and we have also seen, in Chapter 2, that, in general, the absenteeism and turnover rates of older individuals compare favourably with those of younger ones. We now turn to a brief consideration of some of the problems involved in making comparisons in terms of productivity between older and younger workers.

As Welford (1958) points out, the most obvious data which would enable such a comparison to be made, namely production records, are subject to serious limitations.

Perhaps the most important of these is that a marked fall in productivity, or a steady decline, would be unlikely to pass unnoticed either by the employee or by his supervisor, and the result might well be a voluntary or involuntary transfer to other work or, in extreme cases, unemployment. This is likely to mask any age differences in productivity, and possibly also in other indices of work behaviour, such as absenteeism, even when experience of the job is controlled for. The reason for this is that comparisons between age groups are liable to be unduly favourable to older workers, since older people remaining in the job are likely to be unrepresentative of their age group. Thus one kind of selective process which may operate in the work situation can be considered to result in a 'survival of the fittest' (Welford and Speakman, 1950).

A second kind of selection, whereby effective workers are promoted out of a job, may, on the other hand, produce an unfavourable picture of the older individual's work behaviour. It is by no means clear whether these two selective processes cancel each other out, but it is probable that in the majority of cases the former exert stronger effects than the latter. Welford and Speakman (1950) suggest that support for the greater importance of the former selection process is provided by the finding that the variability of job performance measures, in contrast to laboratory performance measures, tends to *decrease* with age. In general, then, age comparisons of work behaviour are only likely to be valid where turnover rates and internal transfers to other jobs are fairly small. In view of these limitations on the use of production data it has been suggested that the examination of the age structure of jobs and occupations in relation to the demands placed upon the worker provides a more useful framework for considering the question of age and job performance, and Smith (1974) provides a clear and comprehensive review of the use of age structures in this context. A number of studies have examined the effects of ageing in industry by looking at the age structures associated with different occupations, on the assumption that those occupations which have lower proportions of older workers than would be expected, on the basis of the age distribution of industrial workers as a whole, will be those which pose particular problems for older workers because of the demands made on their work capacity.

In one of the first British studies of this kind, Belbin (1953) surveyed workshop operations in thirty-two firms and analysed the characteristics of each operation where difficulties were experienced by older workers either in skill acquisition or continued performance. He then compared the common features of the operations on which age difficulties occurred with a control group of operations where these difficulties were not apparent. Belbin was able to show that older workers tended not to be found in jobs involving time stress, that is, where the tempo of work was maintained either by external pacing or by time pressure resulting from a piece-rate payment system. Jobs in which 'time stress' was present contained a steadily declining percentage of workers from the age of 35 onwards, while those in which it was absent contained an increasing percentage of workers above this age. Belbin found that the relation between the absence of older workers and the presence of time stress was particularly marked in jobs requiring training. Training difficulties also occurred from the 20s onwards in jobs requiring a high degree of sensori-motor skill. In addition some tendency was observed for older workers to move away from 'operations requiring continuous bodily movement and activity', especially when external pacing was a feature of the job. In a later study Belbin

(1955) found that a larger proportion of workers over the age of 45 tended to be engaged on heavy and often strenuous work as opposed to light, skilled work in the same industries.

These British findings are consistent with those of a pioneering investigation of the older worker in industry carried out by Barkin (1933) in the United States during the Depression. Barkin collected information on the type of industrial work on which individuals of different ages tended to be engaged, employing five categories of job description. These were: hand work, body work, machine work, clerical work and supervisory and technical work. Barkin found that the percentage of individuals working on body work (defined as 'that type of work which is performed by the application of bodily strength or by the use of tools demanding bodily movements') increased considerably with age from the early thirties onwards. This effect was even more marked in the case of newly hired older workers, who tended to be placed in jobs requiring a great deal of physical exertion. There are exceptions to the findings of Belbin and Barkin (e.g. Richardson, 1953). Richardson found that older workers tended to transfer more frequently from heavy to light work, that is, in the opposite direction from that suggested by the earlier studies. However health reasons (a category excluded by Belbin) or the interview technique used by Richardson (which placed considerable emphasis on the worker's memory for the number of job transfers and their direction) may account for the difference. Nonetheless, Richardson did find that when older men remained on heavy work they tended to transfer to jobs demanding a slower pace.

One of the most extensive studies of the age structure of jobs and their possible relation to work difficulties was carried out by Murrell and his co-workers (Murrell, 1962). These studies were mainly carried out in the light engineering industry in the south-west of England, and began by looking at the median ages of representative jobs in the industry. These tended to be highly consistent for the jobs sampled across a number of different firms, and this high degree of consistency did not seem to be explicable in terms of selective placement. It was found that purely 'physical' jobs, such as labourer, packer and storekeeper, had median ages in the late 50s and hence could be tentatively classified as 'old' jobs. On the other hand, jobs which appeared to make the greatest perceptual demands, such as miller, grinder, borer and honer, tended to have median ages well below that of the industry as a whole. These jobs could, therefore, be tentatively classified as 'young' jobs. Subsequently, job studies suggested that factors in the work situation which were sources of difficulty for older workers were in fact those which did make the greatest perceptual demands. Such demands included the nature of the instructions provided, the type of measuring instruments used, the degree of tolerance to which the work was to be carried out and the size of detail to be attended to. On the other hand, factors such as the amount of physical activity and the size of load to be lifted tended not to pose problems for older workers. Griew (1958) found that older men who remained on 'young' jobs tended to have a higher proportion of accidents than would be expected.

There thus appear to be some grounds for supposing that the age structure of an occupation can be considered as reflecting the degree of difficulty that the work requirements of that occupation pose for different age groups. This hypothesis may be contrasted with the view that an occupation's age structure is merely what Smith (1973) has described as a 'blurred image of an occupation's history', which would reflect such factors as the general conditions of employment when the occupation 'started', the age range of the available labour force and the history of expansion or contraction of the number of workers in that occupation. In an ingenious study Smith (1973) examined these two hypotheses by analysing British Census data for 1961 and 1966. He compared the predicted 1966 age structures of each occupation given by the two hypotheses when applied to the 1961 data with the actual data of the 1966 census. It was concluded that for 133 out of the 188 occupations surveyed the hypothesis that the age structure of an occupation is related to the job requirements of that occupation was superior.

In general, then, it seems that the age structures of occupations differ, to some extent at least, in accordance with the demands they make upon the work capacity of different age groups. This suggests that the interpretation of possible age-related differences in productivity, or indeed, of the absence of such differences, should be undertaken cautiously. Nevertheless, when comparisons of the productivity of older and younger workers in factories and offices have been made, no substantial differences have been found (Greenberg, 1960). It appears, therefore, that older workers are likely to be as productive and to have slightly lower turnover and absenteeism rates than younger workers. Furthermore, although older workers tend to have different kinds of accidents from younger workers, accident rates do not increase markedly with age. The stereotype of the older worker referred to earlier is thus, in many respects, unjustified and the employment problems encountered by older workers can be seen as arising from an employment context in which the pressure on job opportunities is increasing, and in which insufficient use is made of selection, guidance and training methods to enable older workers to adapt to the demands of specific jobs, or – if their skills are obsolescent – to retrain for a second career.

Having examined a few of the employment problems encountered by older workers, in the final section of this chapter we consider some of the problems involved in the adjustment to retirement.

Retirement

Compulsory retirement, is a modern phenomenon and the by-product of the economic, technological and demographic changes referred to earlier in this book. As a consequence of mandatory retirement programmes a substantial proportion of workers are required to leave their jobs when they reach a fixed chronological age, generally 65 or 70, although, as Belbin and Le Gros Clark (1971) point out, there are clear differences in the patterns of retirement typical of different occupations.

On average, men retiring at 65 can expect to live for about another 12 years but their wives are likely to outlive them. Women have lower death rates than men at all ages in all industrialized societies (Spiegelmann, 1966). Furthermore, in industrialized countries at any rate, sex differences in the expectation of life at different ages seem to be increasing.

Whatever the explanation of these longevity differences may be, and there are a number of possibilities, it is clear that their social implications are considerable. In most industrialized societies, the majority of elderly people are women, many of them are widowed and a sizeable proportion of them live alone. The main reasons for this are that firstly, as mentioned above, women live longer than men; secondly they tend to marry men who are older than themselves; and thirdly, they are less likely to remarry once widowed or divorced.

In 1971, there were 2.8m men in the United Kingdom aged at least 65 and 6.1m women aged at least 60, altogether 8.9m elderly persons, 16 per cent of the total population (Wroe, 1973). About 57 per cent of all elderly women were single, widowed or divorced, whereas only about 28 per cent of elderly men fell into this category. Almost one third of all elderly women lived alone, and this proportion had risen markedly since 1951, whereas only 13 per cent of elderly men did so, although this percentage too had also risen quite sharply. Similar trends are also apparent in the United States (Kimmell, 1974).

On average, individuals aged 65 and over have lower incomes than young people and the middle aged, although there is a wide range in the income people in retirement receive. The main sources of income consist, in varying proportions, of occupational and/or state pensions, earnings from part-time work and savings. Income levels tend to be highest for couples and, among those living alone, women tend to have lower incomes than men (Wedderburn, 1963).

Poor health is often taken to be one of the major determinants of retirement, where no compulsory retiring age exists. Palmore (1964), writing of retirement in the United States, found that in his study as many as half of those retiring did so for reasons of ill health. However, poor health becomes a more important determinant of retirement as occupational level diminishes (Steiner and Dorfman, 1957).

The level of general satisfaction with life tends to be greater among the elderly who are still working than among those who have retired, even when health and socioeconomic status are controlled. But, not surprisingly, retired individuals who are in good health and of high socioeconomic status tend to be more satisfied and to have higher morale than individuals still working who do not possess these advantages. Again, a number of studies have found that adjustment to retirement seems to be better among individuals who are 'engaged' rather than 'disengaged'. Engaged individuals are those who maintain high rates of interaction with others, as well as more general contact with the external environment, through leisure pursuits. However, in a well-known but controversial study, Cumming and Henry (1961) examined the relation between scores on an index of disengagement and morale. The surprising result they obtained was that morale seemed to be highest among older individuals who were the most 'disengaged' as well as among those who were the least disengaged from the external environment. However, this result has not generally been confirmed and the theory of disengagement Cumming and Henry proposed, although influential, has not gained wide acceptance.

Although some research has emphasized the psychological problems of adjustment to retirement, many of the difficulties encountered by the retired seem related to either poor health or to financial matters. One of the principal psychological problems results from the social isolation and lack of activity that ill health or low incomes may produce. Nevertheless, some individuals in good health and with adequate financial provision do experience difficulties in the transition from employment to retirement, and part-time employment (even in a completely different job) appears to help in overcoming these difficulties

In order to ease the transition from work to retirement, and to facilitate adjustment to the retirement situation, a number of retirement planning programmes have been developed. Some of these have been shown to exert a beneficial effect on preparations for retirement, and on satisfaction with, and adjustment to, the retirement situation (Fillenbaum, 1971). However, as Fillenbaum points out, little attention appears to have been given to the age at which such programmes should be introduced. She also observes that only rarely do employees' needs and characteristics seem to have been taken into account. Comparatively little research has been devoted to the examination of the effectiveness of such retirement planning programmes and clearly this is an area which could benefit from further investigation.

8
General conclusions

As was noted initially, work provides the individual with much of his status and identity within society. Most people's lives can be regarded as divided into a period of preparation for work, a period spent at work and in relaxation from it, and a period of retirement. As has been seen, much psychological research has been devoted to an examination of the factors determining satisfaction at work and with the relation between satisfaction and work behaviour, as well as to an analysis of the factors governing the relation between the individual and the organization in which he works. Much research, too, has been concerned with ways of improving the 'degree of fit' between an individual and his job, and these include selection, training and work design.

Work, then, is an important element in an individual's life, whether he views it merely instrumentally or perceives it as having a greater significance. Loss of work can therefore be expected to result in psychological difficulties. Retirement, although it is expected and can thus be prepared for, may present some problems of adjustment. Unemployment, however, is usually unforeseen and much evidence suggests that the psychological effects of unemployment, quite apart from those related to the economic consequences, can be severe.

Unemployment retains to some extent a social stigma and in most societies the boundaries between work and non-work are still fairly rigid. If, as has sometimes been suggested, economic, technological and social factors are combining to reduce the amount and kind of work available, then the development of more flexible approaches to work and non-work and their associated life-styles, and to the boundaries between them, will be required. It is to be hoped that psychology can be of help in such an enterprise.

References and
Name Index

The numbers in italics following each entry refer to page numbers within this book.

Adams, J. S. and Jacobsen, P. R. (1964) Effects of wage inequities on work quality. *Jnl of Abnormal and Social Psychol.* 69: 19–25. *101*

Adelstein, A. M. (1952) Accident proneness: a criticism of the concept based on an analysis of shunters' accidents. *Jnl of the Royal Statistical Society 115*: 111–18. *32*

Alderfer, C. P. (1969) An empirical test of a new theory of human needs. *Organizational Behavior and Human Performance 4*: 142–75. *99*

Allen, G. C. (1970) *The Structure of Industry in Britain,* 3rd edition. London: Longman. *11*

Annett, J. (1969) *Feedback and Human Behaviour.* Harmondsworth: Penguin. *86*

Annett, J. and Kay, H. (1967) Knowledge of results and 'skilled performance'. *Occupational Psychology 31*: 69–79. *86*

Arbous, A. G. and Kerrich, J. E. (1951) Accident statistics and the concept of accident proneness. *Biometrics 7*: 340–429. *30, 32*

Baier, D. E. and Dugan, R. D. (1957) Factors in sales success. *Jnl of Applied Psychology 41*: 37–40. *75*

Barkin, S. (1933) *The Older Worker in Industry.* New York Legislative State Document No. 60. Albany: Lyon. *124*

Bartlett, F. C. (1951) The bearing of experimental psychology upon human skilled performance. *Brit. Jnl of Industrial Medicine 8*: 209–17. *83*

Bass, B. M. and Barrett, G. V. (1972) *Man, Work and Organizations.* Boston: Allyn and Bacon. *24, 37, 89, 90*

Bass, B. M. and Vaughan, J. A. (1966) *Training in Industry.* Belmont: Wadsworth. *92*

Belbin, E. (1964) *Training the Adult Worker*. Problems of Progress in Industry No. 15. London: D.S.I.R. *88, 95*

Belbin, E., Belbin, R. M. and Hill, F. (1957) A comparison between the results of three methods of operator training. *Ergonomics 1*: 39–50. *87*

Belbin, R. M. (1953) Difficulties of older people in industry. *Occupational Psychology 27*: 177–90. *123*

Belbin, R. M. (1955) Older people and heavy work. *Brit. Jnl of Industrial Medicine 12*: 309–19. *123*

Belbin, R. M. and Clarke, S. (1971) International trends in employment. *Industrial Gerontology 9*: 18–23. *117*

Belbin, R. M. and Clark, F. Le Gros (1971) The relationship between retirement patterns and work as revealed by the British census. *Industrial Gerontology 4*: 12–26. *126*

Bell, D. (1974) *The Coming of Post-Industrial Society*. London: Heinemann. *13*

Blake, R. R. and Mouton, J. S. (1964) *The Managerial Grid*. *106*

Blaxter, K. (1974) Power and agricultural revolution. *New Scientist 61* (885): 400–3. *13*

Blood, M. R. and Hulin, C. L. (1967) Alienation, environmental characteristics and worker responses. *Jnl of Applied Psychology 51*: 284–90. *56*

Brayfield, A. and Crockett, W. (1955) Employee attitudes and employee performance. *Psychological Bulletin 52*: 396–424. *24, 29*

Brewer, D. W. and Briess, F. B. (1960) Industrial noise: laryngeal considerations. *New York State Jnl of Medicine 60*: 1737–41. *49*

Bridgman, D. S. (1930) Success in college and business. *Personnel Journal 9*: 1–19. *75*

Broadbent, D. E. (1970) Noise and work performance. In W. Taylor (ed.) *Proceedings of the Symposium on the Psychological Effects of Noise*. London: Research Panel of the Society of Occupational Medicine. *49*

Broadbent, D. E. and Little, E. A. J. (1960) Effects of noise reduction in a work situation. *Occupational Psychology 34*: 133–40. *47*

Bromley, D. B. (1974) *The Psychology of Human Ageing*, 2nd edition. Harmondsworth: Penguin. *121*

Burns, T. and Stalker, G. M. (1961) *The Management of Innovation*. London: Tavistock. *112*

Campbell, J. P. and Dunnette, M. D. (1968) Effectiveness of T-group experiences in managerial training and development. *Psychological Bulletin 70*: 73–104. *94*

Campbell. J. P., Dunnette, M. D., Lawler, E. E. and Weick, K. E. (1970) *Managerial Behavior, Performance and Effectiveness*. New York: McGraw-Hill. *57, 102*

Carey, A. (1967) The Hawthorne studies: a radical criticism. *American Sociological Review 32*: 403–16. *98*

Carkhuff, R. R. (1967) Do we have a theory of vocational choice? *The Personnel and Guidance Journal* 46: 335–45. *89*

Carlson, R. E. (1969) Degree of job fit as a moderator of the relationship between job performance and job satisfaction. *Personnel Psychology* 22: 159–70. *25*

Castle, P. F. C. (1956) Accidents, absence and withdrawal from the work situation. *Human Relations* 9: 223–33. *30*

Caston, T. (1973) Patterns of employment and career patterns. In R. Williams (ed.) *Tomorrow at Work*. London: BBC Publishing. *12*

Chaney, F. B. and Teel, K. S. (1967) Improving inspector performance through training and visual aids. *Journal of Applied Psychology* 51: 311–15. *93*

Chapanis, A. (1974) National and cultural variables in ergonomics. *Ergonomics* 17: 153–75. *53*

Cherns, A. B. (1962) Accidents at work. In A. T. Welford, M. Argyle, D. V. Glass and J. W. Morris (eds) *Society: Problems and Methods of Study*. London: Routledge and Kegan Paul. *30*

Cooper, R. and Foster, M. (1970) Socio-technical systems. *Science Journal* 6 (5): 23–8. *60, 62*

Craik, K. J. W. (1948) Theory of the human operator in control systems. *Brit. Jnl of Psychology* 38: 56–61, 142–8. *84*

Cumming, E. and Henry, W. E. (1961) *Growing Old: The Process of Disengagement*. New York: Basic Books. *128*

Davids, A. and Mahoney, J. T. (1957) Personality dynamics and accident proneness in an industrial setting. *Jnl of Applied Psychology* 41: 303–10. *32*

Davies, D. R. (1970) Monotony and work. *Science Journal* 6 (8): 26–31. *52*

Davies, D. R. and Tune, G. S. (1970) *Human Vigilance Performance*. London: Staples. *52*

Davis, H. (ed.) (1958) *Auditory and Non-Auditory Effects of High Intensity Noise*. Project ANEHIN: Final report, Joint Project 1301 Subtask 1, Report No. 7. Central Institute for the Deaf, St. Louis, Missouri, and US Naval School of Aviation Medicine, Pensacola, Florida. *50*

Davis, L. E. (ed.) (1972) *Design of Jobs*. Harmondsworth: Penguin. *37*

Denison, E. F. (1967) *Why Growth Rates Differ. Postwar Experience in Nine Western Countries*. Washington, D.C.: Brookings Institute. *11*

Dept of Employment (1971) *Noise and the Worker*. H.M. Factory Inspectorate, Health and Safety at Work Report No. 25. London: HMSO. *46*

Donaldson, P. (1973) *Economics of the Real World*. Harmondsworth: Penguin. *12*

Drew, G. C. (1963) The study of accidents. *Bulletin of the British Psychological Society* 16: 1–10. *30*

Dubin, S. S. (ed.) (1971) *Professional Obsolescence.* London: English Universities Press. *14*

Edwards, A. L. (1957) *Techniques of Attitude Scale Construction.* New York: Appleton–Century–Crofts. *21*

Fiedler, F. E. (1967) *A Theory of Leadership Effectiveness.* New York: McGraw-Hill. *108*

Fillenbaum, G. G. (1971) Retirement planning programmes – at what age and for whom? *Gerontologist* 11(1): 33–6. *128*

Fjerstad, R. (1965) Is it economical to hire the over forty-five worker? *Personnel Administration* 28: 22–7. *121*

Fleishman, E. A. and Harris, E. F. (1962) Patterns of leadership behavior related to employee grievances and turnover. *Personnel Psychology* 15: 43–56. *107*

Fraser, R. (1947) *The Incidence of Neurosis among Factory Workers.* Industrial Health Research Board Report No. 90. London: HMSO. *36*

French, J. R. P. and Caplan, R. (1970) Psychological factors in coronary heart disease. *Industrial Medicine* 39: 541–59. *33*

Friedlander, F. and Greenberg, S. (1971) Effect of job attitudes, training and organization climate on performance of the hardcore unemployed. *Journal of Applied Psychology* 55: 287–95. *95*

Fromm, E. (1971) *The Revolution of Hope.* New York: Bantam Books. *10*

Gibson, J. L. and Klein, S. M. (1971) Employee attitudes as a function of age and length of service: a reconceptualization. *Academy of Management Journal* 13: 411–25. *23*

Ghiselli, E. E. (1966) *The Validity of Occupational Aptitude Tests.* New York: Wiley. *70*

Gordon, M. S. (1970) Aging and income security in the United States: thirty-five years after the Social Security Act. *Gerontologist* 10: 23–31. *118*

Greenberg, L. (1960) Productivity of older workers. *Gerontologist* 1: 38–41. *126*

Greenwood, M. and Woods, H. M. (1919) *The Incidence of Industrial Accidents upon Individuals with Special Reference to Multiple Accidents.* Industrial Health Research Board Report No. 4. London: HMSO. *31*

Griew, S. (1958) A study of accidents in relation to occupation and age. *Ergonomics* 2: 17–23. *125*

Grigg, A. E. (1959) Childhood experience with parental attitudes: a test of Roe's hypothesis. *Jnl of Counseling Psychology* 6: 153–5. *78*

Grunewald, R. J. (1972) The Age Discrimination in Employment Act of 1967. *Industrial Gerontology* 15: 1–11. *120*

Hackman, R. C. (1969) *The Motivated Working Adult*. New York: American Management Association. *25, 34*

Hackman, J. R. and Lawler, E. E. (1971) Employee reactions to job characteristics. *Jnl of Applied Psychology 55*: 259–86. *56*

Haire, M., Ghiselli, E. E. and Gordon, M. E. (1967) A Psychological Study of Pay. *Jnl of Applied Psychology Monograph 51*: whole No. 636. *58*

Hale, A. R. and Hale, M. (1971) *A Review of the Industrial Accident Research Literature*. London: HMSO. *31, 32*

Henderson, R. D. (1947) Interviewing methods used in the selection of salesmen. *Personnel Journal 26*: 9–18. *72*

Heron, A. (1956) The effects of real-life motivation on questionnaire response. *Jnl of Applied Psychology 40*: 65–8. *71*

Herzberg, F. (1966) *Work and the Nature of Man*. London: Staples. *18, 19, 21, 38, 54, 99, 100*

Herzberg, F., Mausner, B., Peterson, R. and Capwell, D. F. (1957) *Job Attitudes: Review of Research and Opinions*. Pittsburgh, Penn.: Psychological Service of Pittsburgh. *23, 26*

Herzberg, F. Mausner, B. and Snyderman, G. (1959) *The Motivation to Work*. New York: Wiley. *99*

Hill, J. M. M. and Trist, E. L. (1953/55) In J. M. M. Hill and E. L. Trist (1962) *Industrial Accidents, Sickness and other Absences*. Tavistock Pamphlet No. 4. London: Tavistock. *26, 28, 30*

Hinkle, L. E., Whitney, L. H., Lehman, E. W., Dunn, J., Benjamin, B., King, R., Plakun, A. and Fleshinger, B. (1968) Occupation, education and coronary heart disease. *Science 161*: 238–46. *34*

Hinrichs, J. R. (1968) A replicated study of job satisfaction dimensions. *Personnel Psychology 21*: 479–503. *20*

Hockey, G. R. J. (1970a) Effect of loud noise on attentional selectivity. *Qtly Jnl of Experimental Psychology 22*: 28–36. *48*

Hockey, G. R. J. (1970b) Signal probability and spatial location as possible bases for increased selectivity in noise. *Qtly Jnl of Experimental Psychology 22*: 37–42. *48*

Holding, D. H. (1965) *Principles of Training*. Oxford: Pergamon. *86, 87, 91*

Hoppock, R. (1935) *Job Satisfaction*. New York: Harper. *22*

Howell, R. W. (1968) In A. W. Gardner (ed.) *Proceedings of the Symposium on Absence from Work Attributed to Sickness*. London: Society of Occupational Medicine. *29*

Hulin, C. L. and Smith, P. C. (1965) A linear model of job satisfaction. *Jnl of Applied Psychology 49*: 209–16. *23*

Ingham, G. (1970) *Size of Industrial Organization and Worker Behaviour*. Cambridge: Cambridge University Press. *28*

Jackson, K. F. (1967) Comments on Murrell's 'Why ergonomics?' *Occupational Psychology 41*: 12–13. *52*

Jansen, G. (1959) Zur Ensebelung vegetativer Funktionsstrungen durch Larmeinwurkung. *Archiv für Gewerbepathologie und Gewerbehygiene 17*: 233–46. *50*

Jenkins, C. D., Rosenman, R. H. and Friedman, M. (1967) Development of an objective psychological test for the determination of the coronary-prone behavior pattern in employed men. *Jnl of Chronic Diseases 20*: 371–9. *33*

Kahn, R. L. (1972) The meaning of work: interpretation and proposals for measurement. In A. A. Campbell and P. E. Converse (eds) *The Human Meaning of Social Change*. New York: Basic Books. *21*

Kay, H. (1971) Accidents: some facts and theories. In P. B. Warr (ed.) *Psychology at Work*. Harmondsworth. Penguin. *32*

Kerr, W. A. (1950) Accident proneness of factory departments. *Jnl of Applied Psychology 34*: 167–75. *32, 49*

Kimmel, D. C. (1974) *Adulthood and Aging*. New York: Wiley. *117, 127*

Korman, A. K. (1970) Toward a hypothesis of work behavior. *Jnl of Applied Psychology 54*: 31–41. *103*

Kornhauser, A. (1965) *Mental Health of the Industrial Worker*. New York: Wiley. *35*

Kryter, K. D. (1970) *The Effects of Noise on Man*. New York: Academic Press. *50, 51*

Lancashire, R. D. (1971) Occupational choice theory and occupational guidance practice. In P. B. Warr (ed.) *Psychology at Work*. Harmondsworth: Penguin. *77, 79*

Lawler, E. E. (1966) Ability as a moderator of the relationship between job attitudes and job performance. *Personnel Psychology 19*: 153–64. *25*

Lawler, E. E. (1967) Secrecy about management compensation: are there hidden costs? *Organizational Behavior and Human Performance 2*: 182–8. *59*

Lawler, E. E. (1971) *Pay and Organizational Effectiveness: A Psychological View*. New York: McGraw-Hill. *103*

Leib, J. W., Cusack, J., Hughes, D., Pilette, S., Werther, J. and Kintz, B. L. (1967) Teaching machines and programmed instruction: areas of application. *Psychological Bulletin 67*: 12–26. *90*

Levi, L. (1967) Sympatho-adrenomedullary responses to emotional stimuli: methodologic, physiologic and pathologic considerations. In E. Bajusz (ed.) *An Introduction to Clinical Neuroendocrinology*. Basel: Karger. *50*

Levine, P. R. and Wallen, R. (1954) Adolescent vocational interests and later occupation. *Jnl of Applied Psychology 38*: 428–31. *79*

Likert, R. (1961) *New Patterns of Management*. New York: McGraw-Hill. *105*

Likert, R. (1967) *The Human Organization: Its Management and Value*. New York: McGraw-Hill. *112*

Loveless, N. E. (1962) Direction of motion stereotypes: a review. *Ergonomics 5*: 357–83. *44*

Lyons, T. F. (1972) Turnover and absenteeism: a review of relationships and shared correlates. *Personnel Psychology 25*: 271–81. *27*

McClelland, D. C. (1961) *The Achieving Society*: New York: Van Nostrand. *18, 104*

McGrath, J. J. (1968) An exploratory study of the correlates of vigilance performance. In *Studies of Human Vigilance: An Omnibus of Technical Reports.* Goleta: Human Factors Research Inc. *52*

Maslow, A. H. (1943) A theory of human motivation. *Psychological Review 50*: 370–96. *18, 53, 98*

Mayfield, E. C. (1964) The selection interview: a re-evaluation of published research. *Personnel Psychology 17*: 239–60. *73*

Miller, R. B. (1953) *Handbook on Training and Training Equipment Design.* USAF WADC Technical Report No. 54–563. *86*

Miller, R. B. (1954) *Psychological Considerations in the Design of Training Equipment.* USAF WADC Technical Report No. 56–369. *92*

Morgan, C. T. (1961) *Introduction to Psychology.* New York: McGraw-Hill. *67*

Misumi, J. and Seki, F. (1971) Effects of achievement motivation on the effectiveness of leadership patterns. *Administrative Science Quarterly 16*: 51–9. *109*

Morgan, C. T., Cook, J. S., Chapanis, A. and Lund, M. W. (eds) (1963) *Human Engineering Guide to Equipment Design.* New York: McGraw-Hill. *42, 49*

Murrell, K. F. H. (1962) Industrial aspects of ageing. *Ergonomics 5*: 147–53. *124*

Murrell, K. F. H. (1965) *Ergonomics.* London: Chapman and Hall. *40*

Myers, M. S. (1964) Who are your motivated workers? *Harvard Business Review 42*: 73–88. *22*

Neff, W. S. (1968) *Work and Human Behavior.* New York: Atherton. *10*

Odell, C. E. (1970) The trend toward earlier retirement. In P. M. Paillat and M. E. Bunch (eds) *Age, Work and Automation.* Basel: Karger. *117*

Oldfield, R. C. (1959) The analysis of human skill. In P. Halmos and A. Iliffe (eds) *Readings in General Psychology.* London: Routledge and Kegan Paul. *83*

O'Toole, J. (ed.) (1973) *Work in America.* Report of a special Task Force to the Secretary of Health, Education and Welfare. Cambridge, Mass.: MIT Press. *10, 23, 35*

Palmore, E. (1964) Work experience and earnings of the aged in 1962: findings of the 1963 Survey of the Aged. *Social Security Bulletin 27*: 3–15. *127*

Palmore, E. (1971) Sociological aspects of ageing. In E. W. Busse and E. Pfeiffer (eds) *Behavior and Adaptation in Late Life.* Boston: Little, Brown. *116*

Parsons, F. A. (1909) *Choosing a Vocation.* Boston: Houghton Mifflin. *77*

Paul, W. J., Robertson, K. B. and Herzberg, F. (1969) Job enrichment pays off. *Harvard Business Review* 47: 61–78. *55, 56*

Porter, L. W. (1963) Job attitudes in management: II perceived importance of needs as a function of job level. *Jnl of Applied Psychology* 47: 141–8. *113*

Porter, L. W. and Lawler, E. E. (1965) Properties of organization structure in relation to job attitudes and job behaviour. *Psychological Bulletin* 64: 23–51. *114*

Porter, L. W. and Lawler, E. E. (1968a) What job attitudes tell about motivation. *Harvard Business Review* 46: 118–26. *25*

Porter, L. W. and Lawler, E. E. (1968b) *Managerial Attitudes and Performance.* Homewood, Illinois: Irwin. *23*

Porter, L. W. and Speers, R. M. (1973) Organizational, work and personal factors in employee turnover and absenteeism. *Psychological Bulletin* 80: 151–76. *27, 28, 29*

Poulton, E. C. (1970) *Environment and Human Efficiency.* Springfield, Ill.: C. C. Thomas. *49*

Poulton, E. C. (1974) The effect of fatigue upon inspection work. *Applied Ergonomics* 4: 73–83. *52*

Pugh, D. S., Hickson, D. J. and Hinings, C. R. (1969) An empirical taxonomy of structures of work organizations. *Administrative Science Quarterly* 14: 115–26. *110*

Raynor, J. O. (1970) Relationships between achievement-related motives, future orientation and academic performance. *Jnl of Personality and Social Psychology* 15: 28–33. *105*

Rice, S. A. (1929) Contagious bias in the interview. *American Journal of Sociology* 35: 420–3. *74*

Richardson, I. M. (1953) Age and work: a study of 489 men in heavy industry. *Brit. Jnl of Industrial Medicine* 10: 269–84. *124*

Rodda, M. (1967) *Noise and Society.* Edinburgh: Oliver and Boyd. *51*

Roe, A. (1957) Early determinants of vocational choice. *Journal of Counseling Psychology* 4: 212–17. *78*

Roethlisberger, F. J. and Dickson, W. J. (1939) *Management and the Worker – An Account of a Research Program Conducted by the Western Electric Company, Hawthorne Works, Chicago.* Harvard University Press. *17, 97*

Sadler, P. J. (1968) Executive leadership. In D. Pym (ed.) *Industrial Society.* Harmondsworth: Penguin. *107*

Saleh, S. D. and Otis, J. L. (1964) Age and level of job satisfaction. *Personnel Psychology* 17: 425–30. *23*

Sales, S. M. and House, J. (1971) Job dissatisfaction as a possible risk factor in coronary heart disease. *Jnl of Chronic Diseases 23*: 37–45. *33*

Sayles, L. (1958) *Behaviour of Industrial Work Groups*. London and New York: Wiley. *39, 61*

Schwab, D. P. and Heneman, H. G. (1969) Relationship between interview structure and interviewer reliability in an employment situation. *Jnl of Applied Psychology 53*: 214–17. *73*

Seeman, M. (1974) Elusive robots on the job. Review of H. L. Sheppard and N. Q. Herrick, *Where Have All the Robots Gone? Worker Dissatisfaction in the 70s. Contemporary Psychology 19*: 361–2. *9*

Semmence, A. (1971) Rising sickness absence in Great Britain – a general practitioner's view. *Jnl of the Royal College of General Practitioners 21*: 125–46. *26*

Seymour, W. D. (1956) Experiments on the acquisition of industrial skills (Part 3). *Occupational Psychology 30*: 94–104. *88*

Singleton, W. T. (1959) The training of shoe machinists. *Ergonomics 2*: 148–52. *88*

Singleton, W. T. (1969) Display design: principles and procedures. *Ergonomics 12*: 519–31. *41*

Singleton, W. T. (1971) Psychological aspects of man–machine systems. In P. B. Warr (ed.) *Psychology at Work*. Harmondsworth: Penguin. *38*

Slater, R. (1972) Age discrimination in Great Britain. *Industrial Gerontology 15*: 12–18. *120*

Smith, J. M. (1973) Age and occupation: the determinants of male occupational age structures – Hypothesis H or Hypothesis A *Jnl of Gerontology 28*: 484–90. *125*

Smith, J. M. (1974) Age and occupation: a review of the use of occupational age structures in industrial gerontology. *Industrial Gerontology 1*: 42–58. *123*

Smith, P. B. (1969) *Improving Skills in Working with People: The T-Group*. Training Information Paper No. 4. London: HMSO. *93*

Smith, P. C., Kendall, L. M. and Hulin, C. L. (1969) *The Measurement of Satisfaction in Work and Retirement*. Chicago: Rand McNally. *21*

Social Trends (1973) London: HMSO. *12, 15, 21*

Sobel, I. (1970) Economic changes and older worker utilization patterns. In P. M. Paillat and M. E. Bunch (eds) *Age, Work and Automation*. Basel: Karger. *118*

Stagner, R. (1971) An industrial psychologist looks at industrial gerontology. *Aging and Human Development 2*: 29–37. *121*

Stogdill, R. and Coons, A. E. (1957) *Leader Behavior: Its Description and Measurement*. Bureau of Business Research Monograph 88. Ohio State University. *105*

Steiner, P. O. and Dorfman, R. (1957) *The Economic Status of the Aged.* Berkeley: University of California Press. *127*

Super, D. E. (1957) *The Psychology of Careers.* New York: Harper and Row. *79, 80*

Sweet, J. A. (1973) *Women in the Labour Force.* New York: Seminar Press. *118*

Taylor, F. W. (1911) *The Principles of Scientific Management.* New York: Harper & Row. *16, 17, 96, 98, 110*

Taylor, H. (1964) Programmed instruction in industry – a review of the literature. *Personnel Practice Bulletin 20*: 14–27. *90*

Taylor, P. J. (1967) Individual variations in sickness absence. *Brit. Jnl of Industrial Medicine 24*: 169–77. *28*

Taylor, P. J. (1968) Personal factors associated with sickness absence. *Brit. Jnl of Industrial Medicine 25*: 106–18. *26*

Taylor, P. J. (1969) Some international trends in sickness absence, 1950–1968. *Brit. Medical Journal 4* (December 20): 705–7. *28, 29*

Terman, L. M. (1954) *Scientists and Non-Scientists in a group of 800 Gifted Men. Psychological Monograph 68*, No. 7. *79*

Tilgher, A (1962) Work through the ages. Reprinted in S. Nosow and W. H. Form (eds) *Man, Work and Society.* New York: Basic Books. *15*

Vroom, V. H. (1960) *Some Personality Determinants of the Effects of Participation.* New York: Prentice-Hall. *109*

Vroom, V. H. (1962) Ego involvement, job satisfaction and job performance. *Personnel Psychology 15*: 159–77. *107*

Vroom, V. H. (1964) *Work and Motivation.* New York: Wiley. *20, 24, 29, 101*

Warrick, M. J. (1947) Direction of movement in the use of control knobs to position visual indicators. In P. M. Fitts (ed.) *Psychological Research on Equipment Design.* US Army, Air Force, Aviation Psychology Program Research Report No. 19. *44*

Wedderburn, D. C. (1963) Economic aspects of ageing. *UNESCO International Social Science Journal 15*: 394–409. *127*

Welford, A. T. (1958) *Ageing and Human Skill.* London: Oxford University Press. *85, 122*

Welford, A. T. (1968) *Fundamentals of Skill.* London: Methuen. *86*

Welford, A. T. and Speakman, D. (1950) The employability of older people. In *The Aged and Society.* London: Industrial Relations Research Association. *122*

Woodward, J. (1958) *Management and Technology.* London: HMSO. *38, 60, 62*

Woodward, J. (1965) *Industrial Organization: Theory and Practice.* London: Oxford University Press. *110, 111*

Wroe, D. C. L. (1973) The elderly. In *Social Trends.* London: HMSO. *127*

Subject Index